In The Steps Of The Shepherd

366 Short Thoughts for the Long Walk

by H. Lamar Smith

Follow The Shepherd

H. Lamar Smith

10-23-15

Other Books By H. Lamar Smith

Kindle and/or Paperback

The Disciples and The Teacher

366 Short Thoughts for Serious Disciples

Seasons For Deepening The Soul

134 Short Devotional Readings for your walk through Lent, Holy Week, the Seasons of Easter, and Seasons of Pentecost. There are 118 days outlined with 134 readings.

Staying On The Way

366 Short Thoughts for Walking The Jesus' Way

Permissions

Dedication

To the Memory

Of

My Parents

Edgar Horace Smith

And

Mary Lois Howard Smith

To Whom

I owe more than I can ever repay.

Contents

About the Author

H. Lamar Smith has served as senior pastor for 46 years, having pastored in Tennessee, Kentucky, Oklahoma and Alabama.

Trevecca Nazarene University is his Alma Mater from which he received both the B.A. and M.A. degrees.

He has been a teacher of preachers, first in Nazarene Bible College Extension and later as teacher and Director of Alabama Nazarene School of Ministry. Many of his students have looked to him as mentor and confidant.

He is currently serving as Executive Assistant to the District Superintendent on the Alabama North District Church of the Nazarene.

He speaks in local churches for revivals, interim pulpit supply and Faith-Promise services. He speaks in workshops and in spiritual retreats for pastors.

He has three wonderful sons, six delightful grandchildren and two amazing daughters-in-law.

He enjoys writing, building, gardening and fishing.

Devotional Recommendations
(Appearing on *Christ Our Holy Way* Blog Site)

"I look forward to his posts regularly and can say that they are inspirational. He has a way of addressing a Biblical issue and applying it to today's issues in a unique way that is spiritually sound.   I highly recommend you start reading these devotionals."

LeAnn Schmelzenbach Steen
MK, Wife, Mother, Artist

***

"Here are some of the most helpful, insightful, beneficial devotional thoughts I have found.   Lamar Smith thinks with Wesleyan insight, Biblical authority, and experiential authenticity.   I highly recommend these for my friends and family members."

Jesse C Middendorf
General Superintendent Emeritus
Church of the Nazarene

***

"Outstanding daily morning devotional thoughts! Food for thought, fresh daily bread for the soul and spirit, written by a man who understands life."

Lyle G. Parker,
Retired Elder, Church of the Nazarene
Office Administrator at Parker & Parker Law Firm

Kansas City, Kansas

"I've known Lamar Smith since my days as a fledgling pastor of a small mission church in Tennessee. He impressed me as a winsome man after the heart of God back then, and I've considered him a friend and mentor ever since. Each day I look forward to the encouragement and biblical insight I receive from reading his succinct and powerful daily devotional emails!"

Mike Dennis
Pastor Bedford Church of the Nazarene
Bedford, Ohio

***

"Pastor Lamar's daily devotions are short, pointed and profoundly presented. Always scripture based, it gives me food for thought and meditation for my own devotional life. It is a blessed way to start my every morning on the truth of God's Word."

Renda Brumbeloe,
President, Academy of Senior Professionals,
Southern Nazarene University;
Retired Airline Pilot

***

"Lamar's devotionals go straight to the heart of the matter, as if directly from the Holy Spirit to my need. Thanks for your faithfulness, Lamar."

Elizabeth Golden
Christian Counselor

Auburn, AL
"Lamar Smith has something to say and he says it beautifully. For me it is a refreshing word every single morning."

Bob Broadbooks
Regional Director
USA-Canada Region
Church of the Nazarene

***

"Bro. Lamar Smith is a devoted pastor and servant of Christ with a shepherd's heart and a scholar's mind. I look forward to his devotional thoughts because I know they are firmly rooted in the Scriptures, solid in theology and a great guide for applying faith in Christ to everyday life. I highly recommend them as a great way to grow in God's grace."

Rev. Kyle Poole
Pastor, Midland Valley Community Church of the Nazarene
Clearwater, SC

***

"Thank you for your excellent devotional thoughts! They are on-target, inspirational, instructional, theologically sound, even delightful!"

Dr. J. Mark Barnes, Retired District Superintendent
NC District Church of the Nazarene

"I am happy to be on Lamar Smith's 'mailing list' because his one paragraph thoughts & insights are very insightful, easy to digest and a quick read. They are always scripture based. Thanks, Lamar!"

Dr. Jim Diehl
General Superintendent Emeritus
Church of the Nazarene

***

"Rev. Lamar Smith's devotional insights are often just the words that I need to hear. His focus on holy living based in a solid biblical foundation makes them trustworthy guides for the Christian journey. You will be blessed by them."

Roxianne Snodgrass
Pastor's Wife and College Administrator

***

"I would highly recommend the devotional writings that Lamar Smith shares through his emails and on his blog. I enjoy them each day and find them to be encouraging, challenging and scripturally sound. They are very thought provoking as you meditate of the scripture verse for the day! Lamar is a gifted Wesleyan thinker and writer."

Greg Story
District Superintendent
Alabama North District Church of the Nazarene

"Need a morning *pick me up* that's better than coffee? Try Lamar Smith's daily devotionals.   I've been reading Lamar's devotionals for some time now and find them to be inspirational, biblical and they really touch my soul. But they're not all just *warm and fuzzy*, I've been challenged too.   Thanks, Lamar, for this work of love."

John Sugg, Owner
Expedia CruiseShipCenters
Franklin, TN

***

"I have found Lamar Smith's daily devotionals to be succinct, insightful, applicable to real-life situations, and scripture-based.   I look forward to them every morning."

Comer Johnson
Retired Publishing Industry Sales Manager

***

"I love waking up to Lamar Smith's devotions each morning.   I find them to be sometimes challenging, sometimes comforting, but always pertinent.   Starting the morning with God's Word sets the tone for the day and inspires me to move closer to our Lord."

Rebecca Posey
Registered Nurse

"Rev. Lamar's devotionals have joined Oswald Chambers' as my trusted source of daily readings to encourage and draw me upward to higher truths. He is gifted with the ability to capture in a few carefully selected words, the broad and deep experiences of our heart's journey towards our God."

Jenny Hayes
Assistant Director
Nazarene Centro de Refugio

***

"H. Lamar Smith is a unique thinker and writer. He does not indulge in worn out cliche's and past jargon. I have benefitted from his devotional messages."

Eugene King,
U. S. Army Chaplin, Retired

***

"These devotional thoughts have both challenged and inspired me."

Lowell Clyburn
Retired District Superintendent
Nashville, TN

Foreward

These devotional thoughts have come out of my own devotional life over the last several years. Many of these have been sent out as e-mails or included on social media sites. This book is in direct response to many of my readers who have asked that these devotional thoughts be published in book form for regular and repeated readings. I send these forth with my heart's desire that they may be a blessing and a means of grace to my regular readers and new readers alike.

The devotionals contained here are written with the intention that they be short and to the point. It is my hope that they will be a springboard of meaning throughout your day. You can read each of them in about a minute, but I trust that they will be food for thought throughout your day.

May the Lord bless you in your walk with Him. None of us have arrived yet, but we are pilgrims on a great journey with our Shepherd who is leading the way. He is our Companion for the trip and our final Destination!

H. Lamar Smith

Note To Reader

In The Steps of the Shepherd is sent to you with the prayer that these short thoughts would assist you in your long walk with your Shepherd! We are on a wonderful journey with our Lord.

These 366 devotional thoughts can be used as a part of your daily devotionals or as touchstones for meditation. Feel free to share them with your friends.

You have permission to quote any of these individual devotional thoughts in social media or your other writings. When doing so you may use the following statement. "Quoted from *In the Steps of the Shepherd* by H. Lamar Smith, Used by Permission."

Each reading has a month-date indication above the title for those who want to follow the calendar in their readings.

You may subscribe for free daily devotional emails at: http://christourholyway.com

In The Steps of the Shepherd

1-1
Wayward Steps

We followed our own way into the darkness and Jesus found us there and brought us back to the light. We are eternally indebted to the Shepherd who rescued us at such great expense to Himself, though our wandering away was intentional. His love so wants to change our wayward heart and steps. He wants to transform His sheep to hear His voice and follow Him naturally. Oh Spirit, enable us each moment to walk in the steps of our Shepherd.

"I am the good shepherd, and I know My own and My own know Me, even as the Father knows Me and I know the Father; and I lay down My life for the sheep" John 10:14-15 (NASB).

1-2
Our Devotional Life

The Christian's devotional life, among others things, is seeking to live in the conscious awareness of God's presence. Our attention spans need discipline in the barrage of images that assault us. Without commitment to the "one thing needful" we get lost in the trees. Our focus needs daily adjustment. The first step in all of this is a surrendered heart. A heart that is honed in on its Lord, with a desire to be near Him, becomes a devoted heart.

"But the Lord answered her, "Martha, Martha, you are worried and distracted by many things; there is need of only one thing. Mary has chosen the better part, which will not be taken away from her" Luke 10:41-42 (NRSV).

1-3
Rhythms of the Spirit

Life has its rhythms. The Spirit has His rhythms. The art of the Christian life is that we know how to let God blend these two. The Russian saint, St. Seraphim of Sarov, is noted for his statement, "The goal of the Christian's life is the acquisition of the grace of the Holy Spirit." The Holy Spirit makes Himself available to us as we are obediently attentive to work with Him. When we do this, the outcome is beautiful harmony between us and God.

1-4
Inner Voices

Just as there is a whispering voice of God at work in us, we also have to contend with other whispering voices. Some come from our wounded self. Some come from dark spiritual beings. Some of these voices are reinforced by the culture. They seek to imitate God's whisper or they want to drown out God's whisper. They want to program our thoughts and actions away from the good and God's best. Obey your Good Teacher!

"The Lord ... your Teacher will no longer hide Himself, but your eyes will behold your Teacher. Your ears will hear a word behind you, "This is the way, walk in it," whenever you turn to the right or to the left."
Isaiah 30:20b-21 (NASB)

1-5
The Counsel of the Devil

Watch out for the counsel of Satan. He counseled Eve in the garden. He counseled Jesus in the wilderness. He comes to you in both your garden and wilderness. His voice raises questions about what God has clearly said. He offers you another way. He appears to bring new light. He hides His dark motives from us. The best way to avoid Satan's traps is to know the Word of God and the voice of the Spirit with unswerving readiness to obey.

"For such men are false apostles, deceitful workers, disguising themselves as apostles of Christ. No wonder, for even Satan disguises himself as an angel of light. Therefore it is not surprising if his servants also disguise themselves as servants of righteousness, whose end will be according to their deeds." 2 Corinthians 11:13-15 (NASB)

1-6
Let the Light Shine

Good works for the Christian are not a way of showing ourselves off but letting the Light within shine outward. The Light of the World has come to live in us and shine through our deeds. These are the works He would do in your world. We do them, because that is who we are and what we have become. We have this Light inside of us that shines out. Stay transparent, pure and clean so you don't hide nor hinder the Inner Light.

"Let your light shine before men in such a way that they may see your good works, and glorify your Father who is in heaven." Matthew 5:16 (NASB)

1-7
Solutions

It is not easy to accept the things that life deals us. We have to work with what was dealt us or even what we dealt ourselves. It is your reality for you and God to work through. Facing *what is* is the first step to solution. Then know that you have grace-given resources for every life problem. Our greatest resource is Christ Himself. He touches our imagination and we see the answer. Then through His strength we can do all things.

1-8
Courtesy and Respect

There are some basic human principles of courtesy, kindness and respect toward others that are essential in human dialog. When these actions are not a part of who you are, no one is going to believe nor listen to your testimony of lofty religious experiences nor your special insight into biblical truth. If you cannot be kind and speak the *truth in love* then keep your religious experiences and Bible quotations to yourself.

"The Lord's bond-servant must not be quarrelsome, but be kind to all, able to teach, patient when wronged." 2 Timothy 2:24 (NASB)

1-9
Love Because of Who You Are

God loves us, not because of who we are, but because of who He is. We should love others for the same reason. It is not about the object of love being perfect or worthy, but it is about us becoming the kind of persons that will love with God's kind of love. If God had waited until you were worthy of His love you would yet be unloved. God has called us in love to become the kind of people who love the flawed, the imperfect, sinners and enemies.

"In this is love, not that we loved God, but that He loved us and sent His Son to be the propitiation for our sins. Beloved, if God so loved us, we also ought to love one another. No one has seen God at any time; if we love one another, God abides in us, and His love is perfected in us." 1 John 4:10-12 (NASB)

1-10
Refuse to Lose Heart

Life has a thousand ways to break your heart. You must not let even one of them break your spirit. Life with all of it joys has a way of crashing in and crushing us.   In these times we must not lose perspective or heart. Remember, God is in all things working eternal glory in us, renewing the inner person day by day. These afflictions can't stop the glory that God is creating in us. By grace they can only aid it!

Paul said, "We are afflicted in every way, but not crushed; perplexed, but not despairing; persecuted, but not forsaken; struck down, but not destroyed;...Therefore we do not lose heart, but though our outer man is decaying, yet our inner man is being renewed day by day. For momentary, light affliction is producing for us an eternal weight of glory far beyond all comparison, while we look not at the things which are seen, but at the things which are not seen; for the things which are seen are temporal, but the things which are not seen are eternal"
2 Corinthians 4:8-9, 16-18 (NASB).

1-11
Power to Choose

The sovereignty of God does not mean the He predetermines a person's freely chosen actions. Besides that, He put us in a garden and planted all the trees of the garden and told us to leave one of them alone. He gave us the power to choose. God does not always get His way in what happens in His world.   He is always at work in the world.   His sovereignty means that He is LORD even when humans become their own god.

"And when the woman saw that the tree was good for food, and that it was pleasant to the eyes, and a tree to be desired to make one wise, she took of the fruit thereof, and did eat, and gave also unto her husband with her; and he did eat. And the eyes of them both were opened, and they knew that they were naked; and they sewed fig leaves together, and made themselves aprons. And they heard the voice of the LORD God walking in the garden in the cool of the day: and Adam and his wife hid themselves from the presence of the LORD God amongst the trees of the garden." Genesis 3:6-8 (KJV)

1-12
Power of Choice

God has given us the wonderful power of choice. We can choose to obey His voice. We can choose to love Him. We can choose to yield to temptation or we can by grace choose to resist. Choices have consequences, like life and death, joy and sorrow, peace or conflict, etc. We live with our choices, for better or worse. God hopes that we will choose what leads to blessing and not what leads to curse.

"I call heaven and earth to witness against you today, that I have set before you life and death, the blessing and the curse. So choose life in order that you may live, you and your descendants, by loving the Lord your God, by obeying His voice, and by holding fast to Him; for this is your life and the length of your days, that you may live in the land which the Lord swore to your fathers, to Abraham, Isaac, and Jacob, to give them." Deuteronomy 30:19-20 (NASB)

1-13
Passing the Test

Life is full of uncertainties and many trials. We learn to find our way through these things with confidence in God. We are confident that God is in us and at work in us to bring us through these things while shaping and developing character. Uncertainties, tough choices and rough circumstance are tests that develop us. He is refining us like metal. That does not happen without the heat of refining fire.

"Behold, I go forward but He is not there, and backward, but I cannot perceive Him; when He acts on the left, I cannot behold Him; He turns on the right, I cannot see Him. But He knows the way I take; when He has tried me, I shall come forth as gold. My foot has held fast to His path; I have kept His way and not turned aside. I have not departed from the command of His lips; I have treasured the words of His mouth more than my necessary food." Job 23:8-12 (NASB)

1-14
Choices and Intimacy

Your character development as a Christian has a positive and negative component. The negative is that you have to say "No" to some things. There is forbidden territory and forbidden fruit. We say, "Yes" to the good, better and best. Never forget that God has given us more good to partake of in this garden than the things we cannot. Our right choices enable us to walk in close intimacy with our Lord daily. Nothing is better than that.

Enoch walked with God: and he pleased God. (Genesis 5:24, Hebrews 11:5)

1-15
Draw Nearer

God loves and desires closeness and nearness from all, but all do not come near nor live near. A few walked near to God in the Old Testament: Enoch, Noah, Abraham, Moses, Elijah, Isaiah, etc. In the New Testament: Peter, James and John were close to Him. John was even closer. We were made to be like Christ. We were made to be near Him. The true nearness our soul craves is halted by sin, other loves, and a divided heart. Draw nearer and nearer!

"Draw near to God and He will draw near to you. Cleanse your hands, you sinners; and purify your hearts, you double-minded. Be miserable and mourn and weep; let your laughter be turned into mourning and your joy to gloom. Humble yourselves in the presence of the Lord, and He will exalt you." James 4:8-10 (NASB)

1-16
Right and Wrong

God's commandments help us to avoid pitfalls. If God names a thing as wrong, it is for our good. There are things that God has declared good and there are things that He has declared evil. The insanity of our time is caused by creating our own false reality, by calling a thing what it is not so we can make it what we want it to be. This ends in all kinds of craziness. Reality is to acknowledge where we truly are and walk in loving harmony with the God who is at work in us for our good and His glory.

"Woe to those who call evil good, and good evil; who substitute darkness for light and light for darkness; who substitute bitter for sweet and sweet for bitter! ...For they have rejected the law of the Lord of hosts and despised the word of the Holy One of Israel" Isaiah 5:20, 24b (NASB)

1-17
You are the Offering

We are to "present our bodies as a living sacrifice," which is our "spiritual service of worship". (Romans 12:1-2) Yes, our bodies, representing our total being are to be given to Him. This is the same language as Romans 6. Our whole being "presented" (NASB), "offered" (NIV), "yielded" (KJV) to God. Nothing held back! Without reservation--consecration! Full dedication! Believer, climb in the offering plate, you are the offering. Stay there. It is your real worship.

Paul's message on *presenting* in Romans:
"Do not go on presenting the members of your body to sin as instruments of unrighteousness; but present yourselves to God as those alive from the dead, and your members as instruments of righteousness to God....I am speaking in human terms because of the weakness of your flesh. For just as you presented your members as slaves to impurity and to

lawlessness, resulting in further lawlessness, so now present your members as slaves to righteousness, resulting in sanctification....But now having been freed from sin and enslaved to God, you derive your benefit, resulting in sanctification, and the outcome, eternal life...Therefore I urge you, brethren, by the mercies of God, to present your bodies a living and holy sacrifice, acceptable to God, which is your spiritual service of worship. And do not be conformed to this world, but be transformed by the renewing of your mind, so that you may prove what the will of God is, that which is good and acceptable and perfect." Romans 6:13, 19, 22; 12:1-2 (NASB)

1-18
Clean Up Your Road

"Make straight paths for your feet". You can have actions in your life that are stumbling blocks, not just to others but to yourself. It is hard enough to walk the narrow way without all the stuff with which we have cluttered our own road. Clean up your road. Put away bad thoughts, words and deeds. Replace them with the good. This is necessary to walk the highway of holiness (Isaiah 35) making "straight paths for your feet."

"Therefore, strengthen the hands that are weak and the knees that are feeble, and make straight paths for your feet, so that the limb which is lame may not be put out of joint, but rather be healed. Pursue peace with all men, and the sanctification without which no one will see the Lord." Hebrews 12: 12-14 (NASB) (This passage draws heavily on Isaiah 35.)

1-19
The Discipline of the Lord

Our Heavenly Father disciplines His children. He is not passive or permissive. He is not preoccupied with gazing into His universe, but looks more particularly at His image bearers. He loves us too much not to be actively involved in our raising. His love has a thousand ways to discipline us. This, too, is grace! He is not out to break you but to make you. He is shaping His child. Thank the Father today for His correction!

You have not yet resisted to the point of shedding blood in your striving against sin; and you have forgotten the exhortation which is addressed to you as sons, "My son, do not regard lightly the discipline of the Lord, Nor faint when you are reproved by Him; for those whom the Lord loves He disciplines, and He scourges every son whom He receives." It is for discipline that you endure; God deals with you as with sons; for what son is there whom his father does not discipline? But if you are without discipline, of which all have become partakers, then you are illegitimate children and not sons. Furthermore, we had earthly fathers to discipline us, and we respected them; shall we not much rather be subject to the Father of spirits, and live? For they disciplined us for a short time as seemed best to them, but He disciplines us for our good, so that we may share His holiness. All discipline for the moment seems not to be joyful, but sorrowful; yet to those who have been trained by it, afterwards it yields the peaceful fruit of righteousness. Hebrews 12:4-11 (NASB)

1-20
God is Jealous for You

When we are "born from above," it is by the Spirit. Jesus was conceived by the Spirit, so are we at our new birth. The Spirit now lives in us. The Spirit is our DNA connection to the Father and in us cries, "Abba, Father". By the Spirit we have intimate union with God. There is no room for other gods as our lovers. "He jealously desires the Spirit which He has made to dwell in us" (James 4:5).

"You shall love the Lord your God with all your heart, and with all your soul, and with all your mind, and with all your strength." Mark 12:30 (NRSV)

1-21
God is for Us

Life unfolds for us the way it is, not the way we want it to be. Life interrupts our plans. Unexpected events! Shocking surprises! Hurtful disappointments! Expect the day to have unplanned content. You can face problems from your spiritual center and overcome! Taught by the Teacher and coached by the Spirit, you can. Your Father is cheering for you while the Intercessor is praying for you. God has a vested interest in you overcoming all things.

"What then shall we say to these things? If God is for us, who is against us? He who did not spare His own Son, but delivered Him over for us all, how will He not also with Him freely give us all things? Who will bring a charge against God's elect? God is the one who justifies; who is the one who condemns? Christ Jesus is He who died, yes, rather who was raised, who is at the right hand of God, who also intercedes for us. Who will separate us from the love of Christ? Will tribulation, or distress, or persecution, or famine, or nakedness, or peril, or sword? Just as it is written, 'For Your sake we are being put to death all day long; We were considered as sheep to be slaughtered.' But in all these things we overwhelmingly conquer through Him who loved us. For I am convinced that neither death, nor life, nor angels, nor principalities, nor things present, nor things to come, nor powers, nor height, nor depth, nor any other created thing, will be able to separate us from the love of God, which is in Christ Jesus our Lord." Romans 8:31-39 (NASB)

1-22
Be His Arms

Treat every person you meet like a real person. Look at them. Give them a kind smile. Listen. Be present for the other, not just yourself. One way we love the God we cannot see is by loving the people we can see. When we do this there is a sense in which both experience a divine encounter, one in which God is involved. He is present in true acts of compassion. God wants to embrace someone today, but He needs your arms.

"Beloved, let us love one another, for love is from God; and everyone who loves is born of God and knows God. The one who does not love does not know God, for God is love. By this the love of God was manifested in us, that God has sent His only begotten Son into the world so that we might live through Him. In this is love, not that we loved God, but that He loved us and sent His Son to be the propitiation for our sins. Beloved, if God so loved us, we also ought to love one another. No one has seen God at any time; if we love one another, God abides in us, and His love is perfected in us. 1 John 4:7-12 (NASB)

1-23
Our Final Offering

Today we "present our bodies a living sacrifice." The time will come when we present to the Lord the person we have become as an offering. Live your life with that end in view. What kind of person do you wish to present to Him as your worship? Ethically and morally? A pure heart that truly loves God? Love for others marked by acts of compassion, mercy and justice? Life is short. The time of this offering comes quickly!

"For I am already being poured out as a drink offering, and the time of my departure has come. I have fought the good fight, I have finished the course, I have kept the faith; in the future there is laid up for me the crown of righteousness, which the Lord, the righteous Judge, will award to me on that day; and not only to me, but also to all who have loved His appearing." 2 Timothy 4:6-8 (NASB)

1-24
Walk the Way

Be an imitator of Jesus. Know and follow His teachings. Live your life in the way He taught us to live, in your actions and reactions. Let Him be your guide. Step in the footsteps of Jesus. Some days He is way out in front of us, yet we keep moving in His direction. Though we can't see Him, we keep following those steps. He is our coming-to-the-Father Way. You stay on the Way while you walk His way.

"If anyone serves Me, he must follow Me; and where I am, there My servant will be also; if anyone serves Me, the Father will honor him." John 12:26 (NASB)

1-25
Stumbling and the Race

Christians can stumble through temptations in unguarded moments due to pride, arrogance, self-confidence, self-sufficiency, laxness or laziness. When you fall down, turn over on your knees. Confess, taking full responsibility for your actions. Be totally honest. From your knees, cry out to your Lord and Master. From that position you can grasp the hand which will lift you up. Get up and stay in the race.

"Therefore let him who thinks he stands take heed that he does not fall. No temptation has overtaken you but such as is common to man; and God is faithful, who will not allow you to be tempted beyond what you are able, but with the temptation will provide the way of escape also, so that you will be able to endure it." 1 Corinthians 10:12-13 (NASB)

1-26
The Divided House

Humans are broken and need to be made whole. By sin we have turned on ourselves, choosing to be our own god. We have joined the ranks of our enemy and created an alliance which is against us. We are the house divided against itself when we have a divided heart. We need to be made whole. Loving God with our whole being is the "expulsive power of a new affection" driving out lesser loves, and leaving as its benefit an undivided heart--whole and healed.

"Draw near to God and He will draw near to you. Cleanse your hands, you sinners; and purify your hearts, you double-minded." James 4:8 (NASB)

1-27
The New Joshua

The word Jesus in the New Testament Greek is the translation of the Old Testament Hebrew word Joshua (deliverer/savior). Jesus is the new Joshua whose conquest is to "deliver His people from their sins". He enters the heart for emancipation purposes. We have sadly reduced the word *saved* to being forgiven. We need the new Joshua to deliver us from sin by dealing with inherited and acquired tendencies and thought processes from which sin springs.

Jesus answered them, "Truly, truly, I say to you, everyone who commits sin is the slave of sin. The slave does not remain in the house forever; the son does remain forever. So if the Son makes you free, you will be free indeed." John 8:34-36 (NASB)

1-28
Christ's Power

The first step in the 12 Step Program is to confess to being *powerless* to change behaviors solely in our own strength. The second step is to rely on a *Higher Power*. This is not meant to leave God nameless. But is a confession that we need a power higher than ourselves, God's enabling empowering grace to change. The power for the Christian is the indwelling Christ.

"I can do all things through Him who strengthens me." Philippians 4:13 (NASB)

1-29
Stand Firm

He stands above us as the Lord we worship. He stands below us to support us. He stands by us as our Companion on the journey. He stands inside us to strengthen us. In His standing we stand. We stand on His promises. We stand by His grace. We stand on Him as our Solid Rock. We stand up and confess Him before men. He stands up and confesses us before His Father.

"Finally, be strong in the Lord and in the strength of His might. Put on the full armor of God, so that you will be able to stand firm against the schemes of the devil. For our struggle is not against flesh and blood, but against the rulers, against the powers, against the world forces of this darkness, against the spiritual forces of wickedness in the heavenly places. Therefore, take up the full armor of God, so that you will be able to resist in the evil day, and having done everything, to stand firm. Stand firm therefore, having girded your loins with truth, and having put on the breastplate of righteousness, and having shod your feet with the preparation of the gospel of peace." Ephesians 6:10-15 (NASB)

1-30
Fulness

The fullness of the Spirit is mystical, but it should not be vague. The Holy Spirit is simultaneously the Spirit of God and the Spirit of Christ. Thus He comes to indwell us with the fullness of God. Jesus is the image of the invisible God and is the image meant to be the guiding star for how we live. The fruit of the Spirit is the character of Christlikeness and is the real evidence that God lives in us.

"That He would grant you, according to the riches of His glory, to be strengthened with power through His Spirit in the inner man, so that Christ may dwell in your hearts through faith; and that you, being rooted and grounded in love, may be able to comprehend with all the saints what is the breadth and length and height and depth, and to know the love of Christ which surpasses knowledge, that you may be filled up to all the fullness of God." Ephesians 3:16-19 (NASB)

1-31
He is Faithful

Jesus Christ is the true and faithful One. His love is enduring. His grace is securing. His grace is free. He carries our burdens. He breaks our fetters. He lifts us up when we stumble. He never leaves us nor forsakes us. He never gives up on us. He never lets us down. He never stops praying for us. He never regrets His costly sacrifice. He brings out the best in the midst of the worst.

"Your faithfulness endures to all generations." Psalm 119:90a (NRSV)

2-1
Serenity Prayer

"God grant me the serenity to accept the things I cannot change, the courage to change the things I can, and the wisdom to know the difference." Can you have serenity in the face of the things you cannot change? While you are changing what you can? When you are seeking for wisdom to know the difference? Yes! The indwelling Spirit gives us serenity and peace creating a tranquil center from which we live our daily lives.

"Let the peace of Christ rule in your hearts, to which indeed you were called in one body; and be thankful." Colossians 3:15 (NASB)

2-2
Abundant Grace

By grace, you do not have to yield when you are confronted with temptation. If you struggle with a powerful addiction, grace is stronger. When you are beset by weakness, His grace can give you strength. When it comes time to die, you can face it with grace. Grace is *divine energy* given to help you meet life in the strength of your God. Lean on His equal-to-the-moment grace. You will see what mighty things your God can do!

"And God is able to make all grace abound to you, so that always having all sufficiency in everything, you may have an abundance for every good deed." 2 Corinthians 9:8 (NASB)

2-3
The Fellowship of Pain

When you are dealing with the stress and pain of life, identify with the pain of Christ; it has a way of sanctifying your own. He suffered with and for us. We suffer with and for Him. The New Testament teaches that we enter into solidarity by baptism with the One who, by incarnation, entered into solidarity with us. Let Him live with you through what hurts.

You will find mystic union and healing while walking hand in hand with the Suffering Servant. Fellowship!

"And if children, heirs also, heirs of God and fellow heirs with Christ, if indeed we suffer with Him so that we may also be glorified with Him." Romans 8:17 (NASB)

2-4
God Came Low

The One who was above all heavenly creatures, even their Maker, made Himself lower by dying (Hebrews 2:9). This is why exalting ourselves above our fellow creatures insults our Lord. It is not the way the God of the universe acts. The humbling of God explodes our hierarchies. It marks our love for position as ungodly. In the name of the One who made Himself lower than angels, we must cease fluttering around in our self-importance!

"Don't push your way to the front; don't sweet-talk your way to the top. Put yourself aside, and help others get ahead. Don't be obsessed with getting your own advantage. Forget yourselves long enough to lend a helping hand. Think of yourselves the way Christ Jesus thought of himself. He had equal status with God but didn't think so much of himself that he had to cling to the advantages of that status no matter what. Not at all. When the time came, he set aside the privileges of deity and took on the status of a slave, became human!" Philippians 2:3-7 (The Message)

2-5
Lower Than Angels

We are warned not to worship angels (Colossians 2:18) and most of us don't. But, can it be that an undue focus on them pulls our attention away from the One who was made lower than angels? Without focus on Him, there is no worship of Him. He was higher, then lower, now the exalted Lamb at the Father's right hand. He who wore the thorns of mockery and humiliation is now "crowned with glory and honor". He deserves our full and undivided focus.

"But we see Jesus, who was made a little lower than the angels, now crowned with glory and honor because he suffered death, so that by the grace of God he might taste death for everyone." Hebrews 2:9 (NIV)

2-6
Two Antennas

God cares about community and says, "Love your neighbor as if your neighbor were your very self." We know when someone hurts us. But, we seldom feel how our demeanor, words and actions have hurt another. We need two antennas to get clear reception. We already have one tuned to us, but we need one tuned to others. If we are to take community seriously, we must be sensitive to how our actions come across to our neighbor.

"You shall not take vengeance, nor bear any grudge against the sons of your people, but you shall love your neighbor as yourself; I am the LORD" Leviticus 19:18 (NASB)

2-7
Wholeness and Holiness

Holiness is the wholeness and health of the soul being restored into the divine likeness. Holiness is not radicalism, emotionalism, or legalism, though at different times we have made it these things. It is the picture of a formerly divided heart made whole. It is to "will to do one thing". It is love expelling lesser loves. It is the wellness of the soul expressed by "loving God with your whole being". Oh Lord, make me whole in your love! Amen!

"Long before he laid down earth's foundations, he had us in mind, had settled on us as the focus of his love, to be made whole and holy by his love." Ephesians 1:4 (The Message)

2-8
Beyond Feelings

If our Christian life is driven by our emotions and how we feel, we will despair when we are faced with difficulty. When we don't feel like we should feel, we will think that God has let us down. This makes our subjective feelings the barometer of our walk with God. God does bless us, and often times we feel a great awareness of His wonderful presence. But, we do not follow Him for these feelings, we follow Him because He is God's promised Messiah.

"Why are you in despair, O my soul? And why have you become disturbed within me? Hope in God, for I shall again praise Him For the help of His presence." Psalms 42:5 (NASB)

2-9
Your Test

You know that you are having a test, don't you? We observed how Job handled his test in the Book. We watched Jesus come out like a hero. Heaven is watching how you are going to handle this one. Make heaven proud! Don't know how you are going to do make it? Revisit the Jesus test! Wilderness! Trials! False witnesses! Gethsemane! Beatings! Crucifixion! And more! Walk with Him back through it. He passed the test! You can too!

"Blessed is the man who perseveres under trial, because when he has stood the test, he will receive the crown of life that God has promised to those who love him." James 1:12 (NIV)

2-10
Spirit Prompted Praying

When we pray, we include prayer requests friends have shared with us. There are countless other needs which are never mentioned that Spirit prompted eyes will see. Let your spirit be tuned to the Holy Spirit. Travel around with the Spirit seeking to pray for a person or situation at His promptings. We may be aimless, but He never is. He knows why He leads us into intercession. In all situations, He always knows the will of God. Pray with Him.

"We do not know what we ought to pray for, but the Spirit ... intercedes for the saints in accordance with God's will." Romans 8:26-27 (NIV)

2-11
Walking in the Light

Jesus is the Light of the world (John chapters 1 & 9). Paul was converted in the presence of that blinding Light. Jesus is a light path that the righteous walk from night to full day (Proverbs 4:18). For the Christian, the path of light is not an abstract spiritual enlightenment. It is simply that we follow Jesus who is the Light. His Light banishes our darkness and exposes sin. As we walk in the Light, He cleanses us. The cleansed enjoy fellowship with Light.

"If we say that we have fellowship with Him and yet walk in the darkness, we lie and do not practice the truth; but if we walk in the Light as He Himself is in the Light, we have fellowship with one another, and the blood of Jesus His Son cleanses us from all sin." 1 John 1:6-7 (NASB)

2-12
Worship In Your Pain

We have sadly come to expect that if it is not high and exuberant, it is not worship. This perversion has left hurting folks strewn along the roadside feeling even more despair. Ancient Israel had great laments where they expressed pain as a part of worship. It is not a sin to feel your emotional or physical pain before the Suffering Servant and include it in your worship of Him. Don't go down the road of denial by masking your pain and calling it worship. Denial and creating false realities will only add to one's troubles. Simultaneously embracing your pain and the Suffering One is also worship.

"Why are you in despair, O my soul? And why are you disturbed within me? Hope in God, for I shall again praise Him, The help of my countenance and my God." Psalms 43:5 (NASB)

2-13
In His Image

Satan, as *god of this world*, has a vested interest in keeping people away from the true light of the Gospel, which is Jesus Himself. He wants the world to either reject Jesus or think of Him in ways less than He truly is: the very *image of God*. Jesus is the revelation of God, having become one with us in human flesh, so that we might become one with Him. We are being set free to be His image bearers in the world, taking it back for Jesus.

"In their case the god of this world has blinded the minds of the unbelievers, to keep them from seeing the light of the gospel of the glory of Christ, who is the image of God." 2 Corinthians 4:4 (NRSV)

43

2-14
Shared Pain

We find these words strange. "Now I rejoice in my sufferings for your sake, and in my flesh I do my share on behalf of His body, which is the church, in filling up what is lacking in Christ's afflictions" (Colossians 1:24). There is a sense in which Christ continues to suffer through His body, the church. The ascended Lord said to Paul, "Why are you persecuting me?" If I can feel His pain when I suffer, and know He feels mine, it sanctifies my pain for my growth in grace.

2-15
Yearning for God

We sometimes have a yearning, a deep desire, to be at a favorite spot in nature, or with those to whom we have become close. We who have come to know God through Jesus Christ discover close times with the Lover of our Soul through joy in intimacy. We yearn for Him. Never forget that God has a yearning for you also. Be intentional about being with Him. Make quality time for the relationship. He will satisfy your inner cry. He is waiting.

"O LORD, we wait for you; your name and your renown are the soul's desire. My soul yearns for you in the night, my spirit within me earnestly seeks you."
Isaiah 26:8-9 (NRSV)

2-16
The God Who Is

Some reject God because He has been misrepresented in the way He is proclaimed. A few of them recover and come back to see and embrace the God who is, and not the one who has been sold to them. He is not a permissive Father. He does not predetermine every little detail of your life. Nor does He fix everything you insist He must fix. He is not your errand boy. Surrender to Him. He does not surrender to you. Get to know Him! Trust Him! He is trustworthy!

"But you have today rejected your God, who Himself saved you from all your adversities and your tribulations; and you have said to Him, 'No, set a king over us!'." 1 Samuel 10:19a (NKJV)

2-17
A New Inclination

We are born and conditioned to be focused on ourselves. This becomes obvious very early. This inward turn of the self creates all kinds of unhealthy disorder. We need the washing of the soul by the blood of Christ to cleanse and break that bent. The gift of the Holy Spirit in us is meant to bend us toward God, for His Spirit in us is crying "Abba! Father!" The healed heart is one inclined to the Lord in praise, gratitude and service!

"My heart is fixed, O God, my heart is fixed: I will sing and give praise." Psalms 57:7 (KJV)

2-18
A Holy Shaping

Through the events of life, God means to form "those who love Him" by a holy shaping. Life can be very hard. Bad things and evil events befall us. God is not the source of this evil. God has more ways than we can imagine to use all things for the good of His loved ones. The *good* is that we would be shaped like the Son. Beyond anything we can imagine, Jesus had bad and evil happen to Him. Lovingly trust your Father through your shaping!

"That's why we can be so sure that every detail in our lives of love for God is worked into something good. God knew what he was doing from the very beginning. He decided from the outset to shape the lives of those who love Him along the same lines as the life of his Son. The Son stands first in the line of humanity he restored. We see the original and intended shape of our lives there in Him." Romans 8:28-29 (The Message)

2-19
Difficult is a Gift

God is using all things, good and bad in our lives, with one *good* thing in mind, to shape us like Christ (Romans 8:29). Difficult people and circumstance become gifts of God for our character growth, as we respond the Jesus way. To run away is to run from our own shaping. The lesson we most want to avoid is likely the one we most need. God is teaching us to be like Jesus at all places, at all times, with all people.

2-20
Devotion Time

Devotions are more than something on a to-do list. When cultivated properly, these times become the expression of our love and devotion to the Lord. Thinking on God's wisdom keeps us coming back to our point of reference. It clarifies our worldview. My *alone time* with God prepares me to be with others and to be available as a means of grace. Jesus' *alone time* with His Father prepared Him to meet the day.

"Very early in the morning, while it was still dark, Jesus got up, left the house and went off to a solitary place, where he prayed" Mark 1:35 (NIV).

2-21
You and the Carpenter

He is the Carpenter who is always building. He builds community. He builds families. He builds His church, and "the gates of hell cannot prevail against it." He makes Christian gentleman out of crude men. He makes Christian ladies out of loose women. He makes saints out of sinners. He makes victims into victors. He makes over-comers out of the weak. Work with Him and not against Him. Be the Carpenter's helper.

"So then, my beloved, just as you have always obeyed, not as in my presence only, but now much more in my absence, work out your salvation with fear and trembling; for it is God who is at work in you, both to will and to work for His good pleasure." Philippians 2:12-13 (NASB)

2-22
Breaking the Cycle

My friend was embarrassed over his father's alcoholism. Yet my friend became an alcoholic. He started drinking a little alcohol with his friends and soon the alcohol was running his life. He became everything he formerly hated. Unhealthy thought processes and patterns of sin may be handed down from one generation to the next. There is grace to break the cycle with new patterns of thinking and behavior, so that one can be victor and not victim.

"Now for this very reason also, applying all diligence, in your faith supply moral excellence, and in your moral excellence, knowledge, and in your knowledge, self-control, and in your self-control, perseverance, and in your perseverance, godliness, and in your godliness, brotherly kindness, and in your brotherly kindness, love. For if these qualities are yours and are increasing, they render you neither useless nor unfruitful in the true knowledge of our Lord Jesus Christ. For he who lacks these qualities is blind or short-sighted, having forgotten his purification from his former sins. Therefore, brethren, be all the more diligent to make certain about His calling and choosing you; for as long as you practice these things, you will never stumble; for in this way the entrance into the eternal kingdom of our Lord and Savior Jesus Christ will be abundantly supplied to you." 2 Peter 1:5-11 (NASB)

2-23
Your Heart

Jesus is the Great Physician who specializes in heart surgery. He said, "I will give you a new heart and put a new spirit within you; and I will remove the heart of stone from your flesh and give you a heart of flesh. I will put My Spirit within you and cause you to walk in My statutes..." Ezekiel 36:26-27 (NASB). He came to change your heart. You have an appointment with Him. It is about your heart. Please be sure you keep it.

2-24
After Conversion

Jesus calls us in order to cure us. He chose us to make us holy. He forgives us so He can cleanse us. He calls His Bride but then makes her ready for Himself by sanctification and cleansing (Ephesians 5:26). He justifies us that He might sanctify us. He brings us out of slavery so that He might bring us to the Promised Land. He took us out of Egypt but then His deeper work is to take the longing for Egypt out of us.

"Now may the God of peace Himself sanctify you entirely; and may your spirit and soul and body be preserved complete, without blame at the coming of our Lord Jesus Christ. Faithful is He who calls you, and He also will bring it to pass." 1 Thessalonians 5:23-24 (NASB)

2-25
Slaves to Righteousness

"Present your members as instruments and slaves of righteousness" Romans 6:13,19. The righteousness of God is seen as His compassionate action to the weak, helpless and captives. Righteousness for us is to be right with God by way of the New Covenant and expressed by serving fellow humans that are in need. This goes way beyond private piety to concrete actions of compassion and mercy to others.

This is why John Wesley said, "There is no holiness except social holiness." It is a completed love for God expressed to our fellow humans in real relationships such as: feeding the hungry; freeing sex slaves caught in horrible human sex trafficking; helping the helpless; restoring the broken; bringing the lost back home, etc. Wesley also said, "Deeds of mercy must take precedence over acts of piety." This was the choice the pious priest and Levite would not make and the Good Samaritan stepped in to do righteousness at personal cost to himself.

2-26
Soul Health

Spiritual healing comes through a relationship in which we live. Soul health is about soul nourishment, truly connected to the Vine. It includes letting go of unhealthy attitudes that poison the relationship and accepting soul cures through confession and repentance. It is tasting the goodness of the Lord, feeding on His Word, being filled with the Spirit, listening to the inner voice, praising God and having a heart always full of gratitude for your Abba.

"Beloved, I pray that in all respects you may prosper and be in good health, just as your soul prospers. For I was very glad when brethren came and testified to your truth, that is, how you are walking in truth. I have no greater joy than this, to hear of my children walking in the truth." 3 John 1:2-4 (NASB)

2-27
The Discipline of Remembering

Deuteronomy 8 is a call to remember God as the source of our blessings. Worship is the disciplined act of remembering. Without it, God is *out of sight and out of mind*. He brought us out of the house of slavery. He gives us power to earn a living. Abundance can lull us into thinking "by my hands I acquired this". Forgetfulness can take us to exile. Remembering keeps the commandments which expresses gratitude and worship.

"Beware that you do not forget the Lord your God by not keeping His commandments and His ordinances and His statutes which I am commanding you today; otherwise, when you have eaten and are satisfied, and have built good houses and lived in them, and when your herds and your flocks multiply, and your silver and gold multiply, and all that you have multiplies, then your heart will become proud and you will forget the Lord your God who brought you out from the land of Egypt, out of the house of slavery." Deuteronomy 8:11-14 (NASB)

2-28
You Are Loved

The greatest story ever told is that *God loves you*. This story was lived out when God entered into our flesh to pursue us and rescue us. To know I am loved is to feel the warmth of divine acceptance. It banishes my inferiority and insecurity with divine embrace. It welcomes me in creation. It invites me to union with the Holy One. It keeps me from despair. It frees me to love others, knowing I am fully loved.

"This is My commandment, that you love one another, just as I have loved you. Greater love has no one than this, that one lay down his life for his friends." John 15:12-13 (NASB)

2-29
Yearn for God

We have a yearning for the God who made us. We were made by Him and for Him. We find neither rest nor true satisfaction in any other one. Our pursuit of God is a response to His pursuit of us. The God who pursues us is the One who wants to be found, if we will stop looking in the wrong places. When I adjust my quest to how He has revealed Himself and not what I want to make Him out to be, then I discover His waiting love.

"In the beginning was the Word, and the Word was with God, and the Word was God. In Him was life, and the life was the Light of men. The true Light which, coming into the world, enlightens every man.

He was in the world, and the world was made through Him, and the world did not know Him.   He came to His own, and those who were His own did not receive Him.   But as many as received Him, to them He gave the right to become children of God, even to those who believe in His name, who were born, not of blood nor of the will of the flesh nor of the will of man, but of God." John 1:1, 4, 9-11 (NASB)

3-1
Build Solid

Jesus is life's foundation stone. He is a foundation on which you can build your life. "For no man can lay a foundation other than the one which is laid, which is Jesus Christ" (I Corinthians 3:11).   In Christ we can build solid on what is solid.   Satan would have you build on unstable rubble. Is Jesus what you have built your life on? If you act on Jesus' teachings then your life will not be washed away when the storms hit.

"Therefore everyone who hears these words of Mine and acts on them, may be compared to a wise man who built his house on the rock.   "And the rain fell, and the floods came, and the winds blew and slammed against that house; and yet it did not fall, for it had been founded on the rock.   Everyone who hears these words of Mine and does not act on them, will be like a foolish man who built his house on the sand.   "The rain fell, and the floods came, and the winds blew and slammed against that house; and it fell—and great was its fall." Matthew 7:24-27 (NASB)

3-2
The Bible Reads You

When we read the Word of God, it reads us. The Word of God is living, alive by the Spirit and the Living Word Himself. When I am reading it, He is reading me. It is like a sword that is as precise as a surgeon's scalpel. It reveals, judges and corrects heart intent. It is like a mirror that lets us see our inexcusable self. It "reproves, corrects, and instructs us in what is right" (2 Timothy 3:16). Read the word and while you are at it let the Word read you.

"For the word of God is living and active and sharper than any two-edged sword, and piercing as far as the division of soul and spirit, of both joints and marrow, and able to judge the thoughts and intentions of the heart. And there is no creature hidden from His sight, but all things are open and laid bare to the eyes of Him with whom we have to do." Hebrews 4:12-13 (NASB)

3-3
The Obedience of Faith

Paul said that his mission was "to bring about the obedience of faith among all the Gentiles for His name's sake" (Romans 1:5). We have tended to separate faith from obedience. Faith is expressed by obedience. Faith itself is an act of obedience. Faith without obedience is not faith. If we believe, we act on that belief. Faith and obedience are joined as one and cannot exist in isolation from each other.

Even so faith, if it has no works, is dead, being by itself. But someone may well say, "You have faith and I have works; show me your faith without the works, and I will show you my faith by my works." You believe that God is one. You do well; the demons also believe, and shudder. But are you willing to recognize, you foolish fellow, that faith without works is useless? James 2:17-20 (NASB)

3-4
A Healthy Self

Parents often struggle to balance self-expression while encouraging self-denial. The natural self needs to express gifts, talents and ideas. The self -centered self must be restrained or a very unhealthy personality will develop. Self-denial is the only way people can live healthy in families or any other community for that matter. It is at the core of Jesus' teachings. A healthy self can learn to express itself through its gifts.

Therefore if there is any encouragement in Christ, if there is any consolation of love, if there is any fellowship of the Spirit, if any affection and compassion, make my joy complete by being of the same mind, maintaining the same love, united in spirit, intent on one purpose.   Do nothing from selfishness or empty conceit, but with humility of mind regard one another as more important than yourselves; do not merely look out for your own personal interests, but also for the interests of others. Have this attitude in yourselves which was also in Christ Jesus. Philippians 2:1-5 (NASB)

3-5
Healing the Self

A sick self will express itself in sick ways. This unhealthy self can occasionally do wonderful unselfish things, but it defaults quickly to the unhealthy self, and all systems operate from that flawed default. Until this self-system is fixed by grace, good deeds may be a mask for a hidden disorder. A sick self is turned in on itself. The Great Physician can fix that as we yield all the hidden things up for His cure. A healthy self loves God completely and loves his neighbor as himself.

And hearing this, Jesus said to them, "It is not those who are healthy who need a physician, but those who are sick; I did not come to call the righteous, but sinners." Mark 2:17 (NASB)

3-6
How to Treat People

1) You are to treat people like you would like to be treated. 2) You are to treat people like Jesus would treat them. 3) You are to treat people as if they were Jesus. The first is laid down in the Golden Rule. The second is expressed in the modeling behavior of our Mentor--Jesus. The third is expressed in the parable of the sheep and the goats.

"The King will answer and say to them, 'Truly I say to you, to the extent that you did it to one of these brothers of Mine, even the least of them, you did it to Me.' Matthew 25:40 (NASB)

3-7
Hearers Only

Sometimes it appears that persons who most need to hear a word do not hear it, though they appear to be listening. Anything contrary to the grain of their well-chosen ways is filtered out. They transfer the word to others who *need it more*. This makes them feel more righteous. Truly hearing would require saying, "I am wrong," which they will not do. It takes humility bent on obedience to truly hear God's Word and heal the soul.

But prove yourselves doers of the word, and not merely hearers who delude themselves. For if anyone is a hearer of the word and not a doer, he is like a man who looks at his natural face in a mirror; for once he has looked at himself and gone away, he has immediately forgotten what kind of person he was. But one who looks intently at the perfect law, the law of liberty, and abides by it, not having become a forgetful hearer but an effectual doer, this man will be blessed in what he does. James 1:22-25 (NASB)

3-8
Dying and Fruit Bearing

Each spring we plant seeds in the ground that they might *die* and be multiplied. Jesus said of Himself, "Unless a grain of wheat falls into the earth and dies, it remains alone; but if it dies, it bears much fruit" (John 12:24). Paul said that we are "raised from the dead, in order that we might bear fruit for God" (Romans 7:4b). In dying to our selfish self we find a new fruit bearing self. May all of your fruit be like the fruit of Christ!

3-9
Jesus Messiah Is

In a world of detours and dead end streets, He is the Way. In a world of deceit, He is the Truth. In a world of decay, He is the Life. In a world of thirst, He is the Water of Life. In a world of hunger, He is the Bread of Life. In a world of darkness, He is the Light of the World. In a world bound by sin, He is Freedom indeed. In a world of chaos, He is the Logos bringing order out of confusion. In a world gone crazy, He is Wisdom.

3-10
To Know the Lord

Jeremiah complains against the man who lives for himself without concern for others. He reminds him, "Did not your father...do justice and righteousness? Then it was well with him. He pled the cause of the afflicted and needy; then it was well. Is not that what it means to know Me?" declares the Lord" (Jeremiah 22:13-16). To know the Lord we must move beyond our cloistered spirituality to the needy around us. We experience "knowing the Lord" in an intimate way when we help the hurting.

3-11
God Really Does Love You

Bad theology has taught us that God is out to get us, so we are afraid. The God who is revealed in Christ is a God who is in search of all His creatures, so declared by His unconditional love for everyone. You may make Him your enemy but He will always refuse to be yours. His unconditional love for you will never stop. Never! To discover and receive this love is the big turning point in our lives. To celebrate the Father's love is heaven begun.

What then shall we say to these things? If God is for us, who is against us? He who did not spare His own Son, but delivered Him over for us all, how will He not also with Him freely give us all things? ... For I am convinced that neither death, nor life, nor angels, nor principalities, nor things present, nor things to come, nor powers, nor height, nor depth, nor any other created thing, will be able to separate us from the love of God, which is in Christ Jesus our Lord. Romans 8:31-32, 38-39 (NASB)

3-12
To Love What God Commands

"Almighty God, You alone can bring into order all the unruly affections of my life. I pray that You will give me grace to love what You command and desire what You promise so that my heart may be focused where true joy is found. In the name and for the sake of Jesus Christ, I pray. Amen" John Wesley, (quoted in "Ashes to Fire"). To *love what you command*, to fully embrace with joy and without resistance what our Lord requires is real devotion!

3-13
Rejoice With and Weep With

"Rejoice with those who rejoice and weep with those who weep," said Paul (Romans 12:15). This is life changing when we put it into practice. It tells me that, *it is not all about me.* When I do it, I never miss the party. It is incarnational to identify with another. It is community to experience someone else's moment and make it mine. It is solidarity with the human family. It is the imitation of Christ. It is spiritual and mental health.

3-14
Faith And Messiah

The highest form of faith is to hear and embrace Jesus of Nazareth as Israel's Messiah given to the whole world. "So faith comes from hearing, and hearing by the word of Messiah" (Romans 10:17.) From this faith which has Messiah as its worldview and hinge point, then we can build a life of confidence and trust in God who raised Jesus from the dead. Our faith is never center stage, but Messiah is. Love and adore Him and faith will blossom.

3-15
The Radical Jesus

Our quest for easy answers may give us wrong answers. Our shortcuts can get us on the wrong road. We choose answers and roads for our own comfort. Jesus gave answers to His generation that were often radical and upsetting to their ways of seeing reality. He still upsets apple carts and cleanses temples. He meets false hollow worship head on. We cannot radically shape our world without Him radically shaping us.

He entered again into a synagogue; and a man was there whose hand was withered. They were watching Him to see if He would heal him on the Sabbath, so that they might accuse Him. He said* to the man with the withered hand, "Get up and come forward!" And He said* to them, "Is it lawful to do good or to do harm on the Sabbath, to save a life or to kill?" But they kept silent. After looking around at them with anger, grieved at their hardness of heart, He said to the man, "Stretch out your hand." And he stretched it out, and his hand was restored. The Pharisees went out and immediately began conspiring with the Herodians against Him, as to how they might destroy Him. Mark 3:1-6 (NASB)

3-16
Changed by Grace

Never forget where the Lord has brought you from. Remember the sins He washed you from and the guilt He took away. Think of the sadness of what you could be, had you not allowed God to enter your story and change it. Better yet, when you enter God's story, your story is forever changed for the better. You now leave a different legacy than what you would have left. God makes good endings. Thank Him for His life-story changing grace.

"For I am the least of the apostles, and not fit to be called an apostle, because I persecuted the church of God. But by the grace of God I am what I am, and His grace toward me did not prove vain; but I labored even more than all of them, yet not I, but the grace of God with me." 1 Corinthians 15:9-10 (NASB)

3-17
Christ and Your Furnace

Nebuchadnezzar cast the three Hebrews into the super-hot furnace. To his astonishment, he saw them walking around in the fire plus there was a fourth man. When you end up in a furnace, always remember the One who is with you. The God of Jews and Christians does not sit passively by as humans suffer. He is there with us. Christ said, "I will never leave you nor forsake you." A God like that can bring you through anything!

"Then Nebuchadnezzar the king was astounded and stood up in haste; he said to his high officials, "Was it not three men we cast bound into the midst of the fire?" They replied to the king, "Certainly, O king." He said, "Look! I see four men loosed and walking about in the midst of the fire without harm, and the

appearance of the fourth is like a son of the gods!"
Daniel 3:24-25 (NASB)

3-18
The Ministry of Listening

Being totally present for another is a gift of ourselves to that person. So called multitasking and the nature of media itself makes us attention deficit. People want to be heard and they want to feel that you have heard them. It takes focus to hear what a person is really saying. It takes open ears, an open heart and engaged conversation. Being heard is a first step toward healing. Being a good listener can help you become a healing agent.

"This you know, my beloved brethren. But everyone must be quick to hear, slow to speak and slow to anger." James 1:19 (NASB)

3-19
God Loves Us

We are so prone to erect barriers to the belief that God loves us individually and personally. We know He loves others, and we tell them so. But for us, we magnify our sins, faults and short comings to the point that we think He has taken us off the list, or at least put us on the *don't-love-you-as-much-as-I-used-to list*. God is love. His love is irrepressible, unrelenting and passionate. We rest, not in our successes, but in the lap of the Father's loving embrace.

"We have come to know and have believed the love which God has for us. God is love, and the one who abides in love abides in God, and God abides in him. By this, love is perfected with us, so that we may have confidence in the day of judgment; because as He is, so also are we in this world. There is no fear in love; but perfect love casts out fear, because fear involves punishment, and the one who fears is not perfected in love." 1 John 4:16-18 (NASB)

3-20
Let Go of Your Past Failures

God is not preoccupied with your past sins or failures. He desires to see you put all that behind you by confession and through repentance living a new way. So let your past failures go. He is your Heavenly Parent and He rejoices in your growth and character development. He cheers from the side lines, as well as helping us run the race. God is for us, demonstrated by a love that will not let us go and a grace that keeps on giving.

"He has not dealt with us according to our sins, Nor rewarded us according to our iniquities. For as high as the heavens are above the earth, So great is His lovingkindness toward those who fear Him. As far as the east is from the west, So far has He removed our transgressions from us. Just as a father has compassion on his children, So the Lord has compassion on those who fear Him. For He Himself knows our frame; He is mindful that we are but dust." Psalm 103:10-14 (NASB)

3-21
The Mind Garden

The heart and mind is a garden. Some minds cultivate the very things that the commandments forbid. Some minds cultivate the good commands of Messiah. Out of one life comes deceit, lust, hatred, strife, rage, and discord with a whole weed bed of iniquity. Out of another life comes love, joy, peace, patience, kindness, goodness, faithfulness, gentleness, and self-control. In your garden, weed out the bad and nurture the good.

"You will know them by their fruits. Grapes are not gathered from thorn bushes nor figs from thistles, are they? So every good tree bears good fruit, but the bad tree bears bad fruit. A good tree cannot produce bad fruit, nor can a bad tree produce good fruit. Every tree that does not bear good fruit is cut down and thrown into the fire. So then, you will know them by their fruits." Matthew 7:16-20 (NASB)

3-22
The Eyes of God

God sees you. The Eye that sees it all gives some comfort and others fear. God sees all the things you can't see and keep on missing. He sees what drives you; your motives and intent, both good and bad. He sees why you walk away from His prescribed way of doing your life. He sees false humility as the self-congratulatory pride it is. He sees what you are and longs for you to reach your potential as His child. Watch His eyes. They will guide you.

"I will instruct you and teach you the way you should go; I will counsel you with my eye upon you. Do not be like a horse or a mule, without understanding, whose temper must be curbed with bit and bridle, else it will not stay near you." Psalms 32:8-9 (NRSV)

3-23
Faith Is

By His word, God speaks what is *not* into existence. We cannot do that! Elijah spoke it *not to rain* because God told him to do so. He said on Mt. Carmel, "I have done all these things at your word." Out of barrenness, God spoke into existence a nation with the son of Abraham. Abraham did not speak the word, God did. Abraham believed God. That defines faith. Faith is not what I declare. Faith is to believe and receive what God has declared.

As it is written, "I have made you the father of many nations"—in the presence of the God in whom he believed, who gives life to the dead and calls into existence the things that do not exist. Hoping against hope, he believed that he would become "the father of many nations," according to what was said, "So numerous shall your descendants be." He did not weaken in faith when he considered His own body, which was already as good as dead (for he was about a hundred years old), or when he considered the barrenness of Sarah's womb. No distrust made him waver concerning the promise of God, but he grew strong in his faith as he gave glory to God, being fully

66

convinced that God was able to do what he had promised. Romans 4:17-21 (NRSV)

3-24
Intentional Time

We make choices everyday about how we spend our lives. In our humanity, we often lie about what we claim we want to do while we are actively choosing something else. We live intentionally! Everyone does! The real question is what are you intentional about? What your heart is most moved toward is what you are going to do. We will be judged not by our busyness, but by intentionally doing God's righteous business.

"Therefore be careful how you walk, not as unwise men but as wise, making the most of your time, because the days are evil. So then do not be foolish, but understand what the will of the Lord is." Ephesians 5:15-17 (NASB)

3-25
Optimism of Grace

I believe in the *radical optimism of grace*. This means we don't surrender to sin because grace is stronger. Grace can expel from the heart our inborn selfishness, by love entering and filling the heart. One called this "The expulsive power of a new affection." Wrong loves must be driven out. The good loves of life are set in right order by loving God with my whole being. I am radically optimistic about how God's love can fill us up with Christ likeness.

Pray Paul's prayer in Ephesians 3:14-21 this way:
....I bow my knees before the Father, from whom every family in heaven and on earth derives its name, that He would grant me, according to the riches of His glory, to be strengthened with power through His Spirit in my inner being, so that Christ may dwell in my heart through faith; and that I, being rooted and grounded in love, may be able to comprehend with all the saints what is the breadth and length and height and depth, and to know the love of Christ which surpasses knowledge, that I may be filled up to all the fullness of God. Now to Him who is able to do far more abundantly beyond all that I ask or think, according to the power that works within me, to Him be the glory in the church and in Christ Jesus to all generations forever and ever. Amen.

3-26
The Life Path

"I have set before you life and death" said Moses, "choose life!" "Make a choice today about whom you will serve," said Joshua. Both leaders pleaded with the people to make the right choice. Moses said it opens paths to blessings or curse, life or death. "Whoever believes in (i.e. completely trust in, fully relies on, adheres to, stakes your life on, believes into) Him will not perish but have everlasting life" (John 3:16). Jesus is the Path! He is Life!

3-27
Eternal Life

Eternal life is much more than unending life. It is literally the quality of the life of the eternal God that is shared with us. Eternal life is not something we possess apart from an interlocked solidarity with the One who is life (Romans 6:23b). It is the life of abiding in Him and Him in us (John 15). "When Christ, who is our life, is revealed, then we also will be revealed with Him in glory" (Colossians 3:4). Eternal life is our gift inside the Son.

"And the testimony is this, that God has given us eternal life, and this life is in His Son. He who has the Son has the life; he who does not have the Son of God does not have the life." 1 John 5:11-12 (NASB)

3-28
A Place of Comfort

Nursing our wounds; showing our scars and celebrating our pain, only adds to and makes the injury feel more intense. There is never complete healing until you let it go completely. Life hurts. It hurt Jesus. You and Jesus hug on each other and you will get through it. He experienced the full force of pain and unfairness. If anyone in the universe understands what you are dealing with, it's Him. Receive His comfort! Jesus can show you through!

"For we do not have a high priest who cannot sympathize with our weaknesses, but One who has been tempted in all things as we are, yet without sin.

Therefore let us draw near with confidence to the throne of grace, so that we may receive mercy and find grace to help in time of need." Hebrews 4:15-16 (NASB)

3-29
Blessed in Messiah!

Jesus became the curse for us that He might bless us with His Spirit   (Galatians 3:10-14).   Curses are broken by the cross through the Father's love. "The LORD your God turned the curse into a blessing for you, because the LORD your God loves you." (Deuteronomy 23:5).   Balaam found he could not curse what God had blessed (Numbers 23-24). We are free of the curse because of God's great freeing love. We fear no curse for in Messiah we are blessed.

"Messiah redeemed us from the curse of the Law, having become a curse for us—for it is written, "CURSED IS EVERYONE WHO HANGS ON A TREE"— in order that in Messiah Jesus the blessing of Abraham might come to the Gentiles, so that we would receive the promise of the Spirit through faith." Galatians 3:13-14 (NASB)

3-30
Imitating Satan

Once there was war in heaven. A good angel became an evil angel by wanting to be loved and worshipped in the place of God.   God will not tolerate a life

70

centered in itself. The exaltation of self against God and being your own god is the imitation of Satan and his kingdom of darkness. Be humble before God. You are not God. Let God be God. Serve Him with joy and gratitude!

"How you are fallen from heaven, O Lucifer, son of the morning! How you are cut down to the ground, You who weakened the nations! For you have said in your heart: 'I will ascend into heaven, I will exalt my throne above the stars of God; I will also sit on the mount of the congregation On the farthest sides of the north; I will ascend above the heights of the clouds, I will be like the Most High.' Yet you shall be brought down to Sheol, To the lowest depths of the Pit.' Isaiah 14:12-15 (NKJV)

3-31
Your Life Points

God sent the Baptist to point to the Nazarene. Like John, our very lives should point toward the Messiah. A life that points to itself is pointless. It is blunted by asking, "What about me?" The Father witnesses to the Son, the Son points to the Father and the Spirit bears witness of the Son. It is divine to humbly promote the other. Pointing to self is against the grain of the universe. There is fullness of joy in our *decrease* and His *increase*.

"You yourselves are my witnesses that I said, 'I am not the Christ,' but, 'I have been sent ahead of Him.' He who has the bride is the bridegroom; but the friend of the bridegroom, who stands and hears him, rejoices greatly because of the bridegroom's voice. So this joy of mine has been made full. "He must increase, but I must decrease." John 3:28-30 (NASB)

4-1
A House of Prayer

God's temple was to be a "house of prayer for all nations". The word for nations is "ethnos" from which we get *ethnic*. A worship place is open for all races and ethnic groups. Instead, the gentile court in the temple had been turned into a place to sell animals and trade money. It was an *unwelcome sign* for non-Jews. On Monday of Holy Week, Jesus cleaned His house. Jesus wants folks *"not like us"* to be made welcome to worship the Lord of all.

"Then they *came to Jerusalem. And He entered the temple and began to drive out those who were buying and selling in the temple, and overturned the tables of the money changers and the seats of those who were selling doves; and He would not permit anyone to carry merchandise through the temple. And He began to teach and say to them, "Is it not written, 'MY HOUSE SHALL BE CALLED A HOUSE OF PRAYER FOR ALL THE NATIONS'? But you have made it a ROBBERS' DEN." Mark 11:15-17 (NASB)

4-2
His House

The religious leaders of Jerusalem in Jesus day were assigned to keep the peace for Rome. The worship system ceased to be focused on God, but focused on keeping itself in power. It cost Jesus His life for daring to rock that political boat. The leaders found it their patriotic duty to rid themselves of Jesus; to keep what they thought they owned away from Him. He, who is the object of our worship, must also own the place of worship. It is His house.

"Therefore the chief priests and the Pharisees convened a council, and were saying, "What are we doing? For this man is performing many signs. "If we let Him go on like this, all men will believe in Him, and the Romans will come and take away both our place and our nation." John 11:47-48 (NASB)

4-3
Born to a New Life

"He was in the world, and the world was made through Him, and the world did not know Him. He came to His own, and those who were His own did not receive Him." (John 1:10-11) He created humans and came to us but we rejected our loving Creator by forsaking, denying, betraying, and crucifying Him. Some continue to reject Him by ignoring His commandments, not communicating with Him nor taking a cross to follow. To fully identify with Him is to be born to a new life.

"But as many as received Him, to them He gave the right to become children of God, even to those who believe in His name, who were born, not of blood nor of the will of the flesh nor of the will of man, but of God." John 1:12-13 (NASB)

4-4
Thy Kingdom Come!

"My kingdom isn't the sort that grows in this world," replied Jesus. The role of the church is not to establish any political party or system. The church loses its way and becomes corrupted when it does. There is a kingdom present among us unlike the political systems of this world. Christian citizens promote it. It is the kingdom meant to join heaven and earth. So we pray, "Thy kingdom come, thy will be done on earth as it is in heaven."

"My kingdom isn't the sort that grows in this world," replied Jesus. "If my kingdom were from this word, my supporters would have fought to stop me being handed over to the Judaeans. So, then, my kingdom is not the sort that come from here. "So!" said Pilate. "You are a king, are you?... "I was born for this; I've come into the world for this" John18:36-37 (KNT).

4-5
Honor All People

It is way too acceptable to be disrespectful, mean and unkind in how we express ourselves about all leaders. Christians march by a higher standard. We are to honor and respect our leaders and pray for them. You can't really pray through gritted and grinding teeth. Our relationship toward rulers was a subject addressed by both Peter and Paul. Let's pray for the Kingdom of Heaven to work like yeast in the kingdoms of earth.

"Submit yourselves for the Lord's sake to every human institution, whether to a king as the one in authority, or to governors as sent by him for the punishment of evildoers and the praise of those who do right. For such is the will of God that by doing right you may silence the ignorance of foolish men. Act as free men, and do not use your freedom as a covering for evil, but use it as bondslaves of God. Honor all people, love the brotherhood, fear God, honor the king." 1 Peter 2:13-17 (NASB)

4-6
Life After the Tomb

For doing the right thing, you may be persecuted, rejected, maligned, and even crucified. There will not always be a human rescue. Remember, your life is in God's hands. Don't complain about it nor turn it into drama. Leave it be. Give it to God. He is the one who brought again from the dead the crucified Shepherd. He will eventually bring you out of your tomb into the resurrection of new life and a whole new day. Believe it! Live toward it!

"We are afflicted in every way, but not crushed; perplexed, but not despairing; persecuted, but not forsaken; struck down, but not destroyed; always carrying about in the body the dying of Jesus, so that the life of Jesus also may be manifested in our body." 2 Corinthians 4:8-10 (NASB)

4-7
The Clay Jar

Throughout history things of great value have been placed in earthenware containers. Paul gives an analogy of this reality when speaking of believers as jars of clay and light bearers. The jar holds the oil and wick. The greater thing is the light that glows from the clay jar. O clay jar, you have been chosen to be a bearer of the great treasure called Jesus the Light. Tend the divine Light. Let Him glow so brightly that they don't even notice the jar.

For God, who said, "Let light shine out of darkness," made his light shine in our hearts to give us the light of the knowledge of the glory of God in the face of Christ. But we have this treasure in jars of clay to show that this all-surpassing power is from God and not from us. 2 Corinthians 4:6-7 (NIV)

4-8
What to Do and Be

"The one who abides in love abides in God, and God abides in him...*because as He is, so also are we in this world*" I John 4:16b, 17b (NASB). Being in the world like Jesus was in the world is our mission. He was here as: love to embrace; compassion to restore; seeker of the lost; healer of the found; forgiver of enemies; captive releaser; hungry feeder; slave to serve; living image of God and more. Now we know what we are to be and do!

4-9
Identity and Acceptance

It is possible to look for love in all the wrong places. One example is when our thirst entices us to drink from polluted pools. It is probable that these drives can bring us to people who redefine our identity and shape us in very negative ways. In the company of Jesus, the disciples found an identity as being the children of a loving Heavenly Father and citizens of the Kingdom of God. In Jesus, I too, have found who I am.

"Behold what manner of love the Father bestowed upon us, that we should be called the children of God" (I John 3:1).

4-10
Processing

When we are committed to daily devotional readings, we must remember why we do it. We must not hurriedly scan the words, so that we can say, "I had my devotions." We are to read with a thoughtful meditative mind for purposes of worship and personal growth. We must process what we read, and let it process us. In this way we will possess what we read because it has become a part of us. It is then that we have grown in our devotion to our Lord.

How blessed is the man who does not walk in the counsel of the wicked, Nor stand in the path of sinners, Nor sit in the seat of scoffers! But his delight

is in the law of the Lord, And in His law he meditates day and night.
He will be like a tree firmly planted by streams of water, which yields its fruit in its season And its leaf does not wither; And in whatever he does, he prospers. Psalm 1:1-3 (NASB)

4-11
Shine Where You Are

You can choose to make your bad circumstances a place for a deeper consecration. Our circumstances don't define us. Our choices do. In Christ we are not victims but victors. We have nothing to whine about. We can even rejoice in the midst of suffering. Surrender to the refiner's fire, and it can make your worst day your best day. Fire changes ugly ore into shining silver or gold, able to reflect the righteous image of the Refiner.

"He is like a refiner's fire and like fuller soap. And He will sit as a smelter and purifier of silver, and He will purify the sons of Levi and refine them like gold and silver, so that they may present to the Lord offerings in righteousness." Malachi 3:2b-3 (NASB)

4-12
His Image Bearers

In ancient times, a king who extended his kingdom would erect an image of himself in his newly acquired territory. The people of God are the image of God in the world. We are *chosen* as His people to reclaim what is already His. "All the earth is mine" (see Exodus 19:3-6). He is reclaiming creation by those who bear the image of His Son even now. Represent Him well! Have you taken back any territory of your King lately?

"Beloved, I urge you as aliens and strangers to abstain from fleshly lusts which wage war against the soul. Keep your behavior excellent among the Gentiles, so that in the thing in which they slander you as evildoers, they may because of your good deeds, as they observe them, glorify God in the day of visitation." 1 Peter 2:11-12 (NASB)

4-13
Second-Mile People

Some things we do are our normal duty. Other things are those creative things of doing more than is required. All around us we see those who live by doing the least. "That's all I get paid for", they say. They do their *duty* and no more, and with no joy. Then there is the joy-filled second-mile way to live by doing the extra. Serve all as you would serve the Lord Himself, for He comes to you "as the least of these".

"So you too, when you do all the things which are commanded you, say, 'We are unworthy servants; we have done only that which we ought to have done.' " Luke 17:10 (NASB)

4-14
God is Revealed

Without the fullness of the revelation of God in Jesus Christ, we would be left to speculation about the nature of God. The revelation of the Old Testament was partial and incomplete.   The revelation of the New Testament is full and final. God now says to us by His Spirit what He has already said through the revelation of His Son, our Messiah. He has no more that He can say to us than that. This is the message that cannot to be added to and is perilous to diminish. We have not yet plumbed its depths nor explored its heights.

"God, after He spoke long ago to the fathers in the prophets in many portions and in many ways, in these last days has spoken to us in His Son, whom He appointed heir of all things, through whom also He made the world. And He is the radiance of His glory and the exact representation of His nature, and upholds all things by the word of His power. When He had made purification of sins, He sat down at the right hand of the Majesty on high, having become as much better than the angels, as He has inherited a more excellent name than they." Hebrews 1:1-4 (NASB)

4-15
Grace to Help

There is a place to go when you need mercy and "grace to help in time of need". It is to Jesus the Son of God, seated at the right hand of the Father as the interceding High Priest. We are needy creatures who always need mercy and "grace to help". This grace is more than *unmerited favor*, it is *unmerited energy* that keeps giving strength in all we do.   Grace is God's daily commitment to you.

"Therefore, since we have a great high priest who has passed through the heavens, Jesus the Son of God, let us hold fast our confession. For we do not have a high priest who cannot sympathize with our weaknesses, but One who has been tempted in all things as we are, yet without sin.   Therefore let us draw near with confidence to the throne of grace, so that we may receive mercy and find grace to help in time of need." Hebrews 4:14-16 (NASB)

4-16
The To-Do List

Life just might explode with new purpose and meaning if we asked God what is on His to-do list for us, instead of us giving Him our to-do list each morning.   "What would you have me to do, Lord?" When we see something good and compassionate that needs to be done, has He not already spoken to our ears through our eyes?

Then the Lord came and stood and called as at other times, "Samuel! Samuel!" And Samuel said, "Speak, for Your servant is listening." 1 Samuel 3:10 (NASB)

4-17
Triumph Even In Sorrow

In the midst of the joys of life we often experience heavy sorrows. In the midst of the sorrows of life we often experience great joys. In the midst of it all, God is still God. His people are still His people. We own Him. He owns us. We are in Him. He is in us. So come what may, God through you will triumph. He will do more than you ever dreamed He could.

"What then shall we say to these things? If God is for us, who is against us?" Romans 8:31 (NASB)

4-18
Fresh Grace

His grace and compassion are new and fresh each morning. Our relationship with God is not static but dynamic. It is not mechanical but organic. God is forever creating new ways to show grace to His creatures. Fresh grace is the manna we gather every day. It is sufficient, strengthening and satisfying. Taste and see!

"The Lord's lovingkindnesses indeed never cease, For His compassions never fail. They are new every morning; Great is Your faithfulness." Lamentations 3:22-23 (NASB)

4-19
Givers of Grace

No one deserves grace. Yet the Nazarene taught us that God is a lavish giver of grace and we are to give grace freely as He has given to us. Being a giver of grace is one way we are the image bearers of God where we are planted. Givers of unconditional love and grace mark us as His. Some people will resist or reject grace. It happens to God all the time. Yet we must keep on giving, finding creative new ways to show grace.

"You have heard that it was said, 'You shall love your neighbor and hate your enemy.' But I say to you, love your enemies and pray for those who persecute you, so that you may be sons of your Father who is in heaven; for He causes His sun to rise on the evil and the good, and sends rain on the righteous and the unrighteous. For if you love those who love you, what reward do you have? Do not even the tax collectors do the same? If you greet only your brothers, what more are you doing than others? Do not even the Gentiles do the same? Therefore you are to be perfect, as your heavenly Father is perfect." Matthew 5:43-48 (NASB)

4-20
The Creator's Hand

God created the world and by Him all things hold together. It seems that some TV programming is always trying to scare us about some possible cosmic random event hitting the earth from space. His hand is on His creation protecting it from utter chaos. The Creator's hand has not gone away. His hand is on your life, too, working to bring order, purpose and meaning. Trust your life completely to that Hand.

"For by Him all things were created, both in the heavens and on earth, visible and invisible, whether thrones or dominions or rulers or authorities—all things have been created through Him and for Him. He is before all things, and in Him all things hold together." Colossians 1:16-17 (NASB)

4-21
More Than We Can Imagine

Though the Messiah was prophesied in the OT, yet He came in ways they could not have imagined. If we had never seen corn, we could never imagine that there would be a grass that would grow so tall with such large and abundant fruit. Who knew that Messiah would be Isaiah's Suffering Servant, Lamb of God, Creator Incarnate? And on and on we could go. He is more than we will ever be able to put our minds around.

"What was from the beginning, what we have heard, what we have seen with our eyes, what we have looked at and touched with our hands, concerning the Word of Life—and the life was manifested, and we have seen and testify and proclaim to you the eternal life, which was with the Father and was manifested to us- what we have seen and heard we proclaim to you also, so that you too may have fellowship with us; and indeed our fellowship is with the Father, and with His Son Jesus Christ." 1 John 1:1-3 (NASB)

4-22
Temptation in Culture

We know that the line between temptation and sin is yielding. However, there is a yielding to temptation that does not feel like yielding. It is conforming our actions to the peer pressure aspects of culture, which, when examined prove to be unchristian. Satan wraps himself in the cloak of culture in systemic ways. We must resist the unchristian aspects of culture as subtle forms of temptation, which they are.

"Submit therefore to God. Resist the devil and he will flee from you. Draw near to God and He will draw near to you. Cleanse your hands, you sinners; and purify your hearts, you double-minded." James 4:7-8 (NASB)

4-23
Doing Good

You cannot do bad and then feel good about yourself. Do good and feel good about yourself as a follower of Messiah. Doing the right thing, as He defines right, can make you feel good about the person you are becoming. Beyond that is an assurance that you have pleased the Father. We hear a whisper in our spirit of "Well done, my child." Now that's a blessing of affirmation about which we should feel good!

"How blessed are those whose way is blameless, Who walk in the law of the Lord. How blessed are those who observe His testimonies, Who seek Him with all their heart. They also do no unrighteousness; They walk in His ways. You have ordained Your precepts, That we should keep them diligently. Oh that my ways may be established To keep Your statutes! Then I shall not be ashamed When I look upon all Your commandments."
Psalm 119:1-6 (NASB)

4-24
A Christian

A Christian is one who follows the teachings of Jesus. These are His disciples, His apprentices. Being a Christian is much more than reciting the right formula. His true followers love Him and are serious about keeping His commandments in their thoughts, words and deeds. His teaching will change all of our thoughts, how we say our words and will be the well spring of all our deeds. Christians are those who live out His life changing words.

"He who has My commandments and keeps them is the one who loves Me; and he who loves Me will be loved by My Father, and I will love him and will disclose Myself to him." John 14:21 (NASB)

4-25
One Step at a Time

God, in His ever active creative powers, has answers to our problems. He is waiting for us to discover them. Sometimes it takes searching. Sometimes it takes waiting. All the time it requires listening with willing hands and a surrendered heart. Most of the time, we discover the answer one step at a time. As we do the first thing, not sure of what is next, He keeps leading. When we finish, we look back and know, "God did that."

"Our steps are made firm by the Lord, when he delights in our way; though we stumble, we shall not fall headlong, for the Lord holds us by the hand." Psalm 37:23-24 (NRSV)

4-26
The Father and Community

When we disobey our Father, we want to go and hide from Him. Sin interferes with the relationship, not only with our Father, but with everyone who is in this garden with us. There is no isolated disobedience. It hurts the community because it changes the persons we are in the community. When we are rightly related to our Father, we are eager for time with Him and become a better person for the other people in our lives.

They heard the sound of the Lord God walking in the garden in the cool of the day, and the man and his wife hid themselves from the presence of the Lord

God among the trees of the garden. Then the Lord God called to the man, and said to him, "Where are you?" He said, "I heard the sound of You in the garden, and I was afraid because I was naked; so I hid myself." Genesis 3:8-10 (NASB)

4-27
The Intercessor

"Satan desires to sift you like wheat, but I have prayed for you that your faith fail not" (Luke 22:31-32). Make no doubt that our Intercessor prays a similar prayer for us in times of Satanic attacks. Satan is a master manipulator, trying to take us away from faith, one step at a time. As you struggle through times of testing, listen in on the heavenly Intercessor and hear Him praying for you.

"He is able also to save forever those who draw near to God through Him, since He always lives to make intercession for them." Hebrews 7:25 (NASB)

4-28
Because of Who You Have Become

The best ministry is that which flows from who you are. It is natural and you don't even think about it. This is serving that springs up from transformed character. It is sheep "doing unto the least of these," not because they had it figured out, but because it was their sheep nature to do so (Matt 25:31-46). He judges us by our deeds for they are the fruit of the person we have become.

4-29
Obedience as Worship

Someone said long ago, "Partial obedience is disobedience." It is difficult for us to get clear answers and direction for our lives while in disobedience to the teachings of Christ. Light become darkness when it is not coupled with obedience. Full, immediate, non-hesitating obedience should be our pattern. Obedience is better than our sacrifices. Without it our worship is not worship.

Samuel said, "Has the Lord as much delight in burnt offerings and sacrifices As in obeying the voice of the Lord? Behold, to obey is better than sacrifice, And to heed than the fat of rams. "For rebellion is as the sin of divination, And insubordination is as iniquity and idolatry." 1 Samuel 15:22-23a (NASB)

4-30
Wisdom

None is more foolish than the one who is his own teacher. He lives subjectively with no external correction system. He is bound to make countless mistakes, because he does not draw from the wisdom of others. It is much better to embrace the accumulated wisdom of the human family and learn to sit at the feet of the wise. It is better still to sit at the feet of the greatest Teacher of all times. He is truly the Wisdom of God.

Simon Peter answered Him, "Lord, to whom shall we go? You have words of eternal life. We have believed and have come to know that You are the Holy One of God." John 6:68-69 (NASB)

5-1
Character Development

The Father sees things in His children that need correcting but that are not yet on our field of view. He has great compassion for us, but He is not the permissive parent. He is vigilant to accomplish our character development. Self-discipline means that we have become "workers together with God" in the person we are becoming.

"For I am confident of this very thing, that He who began a good work in you will perfect it until the day of Christ Jesus." Philippians 1:6 (NASB)

5-2
Breaking Chains

If God is trying to break the chains of your bondage, don't keep adding links. Help Him dismantle the thing. Undisciplined behavior makes you even more undisciplined. Don't bring into your life that which you know contributes to your bondage. There is power great enough to make you free, but seldom does God bring it without tough character building decisions on our part. Work with Him.

"It was for freedom that Christ set us free; therefore keep standing firm and do not be subject again to a yoke of slavery." Galatians 5:1 (NASB)

5-3
The Lamb Won

God was upset about all the violence in the world so He sent a Lamb to fix it. He could have said, "All those people understand is power, so I will hit them hard." The Lamb did not come in power but weakness. They killed the Precious Lamb. He never opened His mouth in protest. Weakness won over power, love over meanness. The Lamb is Victor! The Serpent has the hoof prints of the Lamb on his crushed head.

"When He had disarmed the rulers and authorities, He made a public display of them, having triumphed over them through Him." Galatians 5:1 (NASB)

5-4
To Be Available

Praying without praise and thanksgiving turns our prayers into a God-to-do list. Praying without listening and quietness turns our prayers into talking out what we want but never listening to see what God wants. Praying is not for us to use God for our ends but for God to use us for His ends. Samuel said, "Speak Lord, your servant is listening" (I Samuel 3:10). In Hebrews, listening means *Available*. God is looking for the available.

5-5
Temperance

Self-control or temperance is a Christian virtue and includes discipline in what we eat and how much we eat. Our stomachs stretch to adjust to the quantities we consume. When we overeat our body tells us that is how much we need the next time. Our god is not our belly (Philippians 3:19). Discipline all of your appetites as well as your attitudes. This is the message of self-control and temperance.

"For the overseer must be above reproach as God's steward, not self-willed, not quick-tempered, not addicted to wine, not pugnacious, not fond of sordid gain, but hospitable, loving what is good, sensible, just, devout, self-controlled, holding fast the faithful word which is in accordance with the teaching, so that he will be able both to exhort in sound doctrine and to refute those who contradict." Titus 1:7-9 (NASB)

5-6
Worship Time

We have an adversary who is ever finding new ways to keep believers away from worship. He will even convince you that his ideas for the weekend are better for your family than "being in church all the time." He has a plan. It is to break the consistent church habit and replace it with other things. It is to take the focus away from the centrality of the Christ in worship to the worship of leisure. It moves families and nations away from God. The adversary's plan is working in too many places. Be careful!

"Not forsaking our own assembling together, as is the habit of some, but encouraging one another; and all the more as you see the day drawing near." Hebrews 10:25 (NASB)

5-7
Relying on God

There is a huge difference between believing that God exists and relying on God. We go through our days as if He does not exist, becoming practical atheist. The demons believe that God exists "and tremble". As Wesley said, "They believe and are demons still." Is the faith that believes in God and does not tremble, a faith that is lower than that of the demons? Hold your Father in great awe and worship, relying on His grace every day.

"You believe that God is one. You do well; the demons also believe, and shudder." James 2:19 (NASB)

5-8
To Love Completely

Moses led the people out of Egypt but struggled with how he could get Egypt out of the people. They wanted to go back to its delicacies. It is one thing for God to rescue us out of sin and it is yet another thing for us to deal with our bent toward sin. The indwelling Holy Spirit sheds abroad the love of God in our hearts, giving us what one has called, "The expulsive power of a new affection." To love God completely drives out lesser loves.

"And hope does not disappoint, because the love of God has been poured out within our hearts through the Holy Spirit who was given to us." Romans 5:5 (NASB)

5-9
Get Stronger

"Nevertheless the righteous will hold to His way, and he who has clean hands will grow stronger and stronger" (Job 17:9 NASB). *Clean hands* refers to acts of righteousness and compassion. Dirty hands would be to have on our hands neglect or abuse of other humans. God's strength flows through the arm and hand that comes to the aid of those in need. We get stronger when we help the weak.

5-10
Receiving Love's Initiative

All persons are objects of God's love. We must not confuse God's love for all as salvation for all. Transformation comes as we embrace God's unconditional love. Its greatest display is the cross. We receive it, we enter it, it enters us and we live from it. This love we have embraced becomes evident when we give it back to God and freely give it to others. This is the mark of those in the salvation community.

"Whoever believes that Jesus is the Christ is born of God, and whoever loves the Father loves the child born of Him. By this we know that we love the children of God, when we love God and observe His commandments. For this is the love of God, that we keep His commandments; and His commandments are not burdensome. For whatever is born of God overcomes the world; and this is the victory that has overcome the world—our faith. Who is the one who overcomes the world, but he who believes that Jesus is the Son of God? 1 John 5:1-5 (NASB)

5-11
Joy

The self-absorbed celebrate their neglect by others. They do not know how to center on another, and find joy in it. They refuse to "rejoice with those who rejoice and weep with those who weep." They will not sing another's song. So they have not yet found the joy of losing oneself and finding a cleansed self. Joy comes from a right relationship to God and the other people in my life. It is how I relate. It is not in getting but giving.

"Let each of you look not to your own interests, but to the interests of others." Philippians 2:4 (NRSV)

5-12
Be Holy

"But just as he who called you is holy, so be holy in all you do; for it is written: 'Be holy, because I am holy'" 1 Peter 1:15-16 (NIV). We are commanded to be like God. The inner and outer workings of the Spirit in us make it possible. We are to be "holy in all we do". Holy habits shape holy character. A cleansed heart learns to do holy things. The cleansing of our inner self and actions of love expressed to God and neighbor is holiness.

5-13
A Holy Chase

"Let us also lay aside every encumbrance and the sin which so easily entangles us, and let us run with endurance the race that is set before us, fixing our eyes on Jesus....run after peace with all men, and the sanctification without which no one will see the Lord" Hebrews 12:1-2, 14 (NASB). You run to and toward Jesus for your sanctification. You need more of Him and He needs all of you. "Strengthen your feeble knees and run" (v.12).

5-14
Forgive Me

Human relationships can cause unintentional hurts. If we would be honest, we too have been the cause of another's pain. We can't know that in our self-focus. We can only know it by sensitivity toward another. I exist not merely in my own world but in the world of others. When I bump into another, politeness says, "Pardon me." When I have hurt or offended another, the right words are, "Forgive me." Two powerfully healing words.

"As God's chosen ones, holy and beloved, clothe yourselves with compassion, kindness, humility, meekness, and patience. Bear with one another and, if anyone has a complaint against another, forgive each other; just as the Lord has forgiven you, so you also must forgive." Colossians 3:12-13 (NRSV)

5-15
The Will of God

"This is the will of God, even your sanctification that you abstain from sexual immorality" I Thessalonians 4:3 (NASB). The will of God is that I would be a person of moral purity. We want to find God's will in *what to do* while neglecting *what to be*. God's will is concerned first with the kind of person you are and second with what you do. Good habits of *doing* can shape the character of *being*. And *being* right will help to shape the *doing*.

5-16
Be Right

Righteousness is right relationship to God based on the terms He has offered. He offers us a relationship to Himself through His Son.   Faith, trust and confidence in Jesus the Messiah of the kingdom of God, and to live your life in that reality is the relationship we enter. This offer from God is a free gift. Our relationship with others is an action. God will reward those, who by their living, demonstrate righteousness (Matthew 25).

5-17
Do Right

The Righteousness of God is God's compassionate mercy and restorative justice in action. This is the right relationship that the Creator Father God has with His creatures. Since this is how He relates to us, and since we are to be like God, then we are commanded to relate to everyone else with God's kind of compassionate mercy and restorative justice. In this way, we express the righteousness of God as His image bearers in creation.

"LORD, who may dwell in your sanctuary? Who may live on your holy hill? He whose walk is blameless and who does what is righteous, who speaks the truth from his heart." Psalms 15:1-2 (NIV)

5-18
Our City

Abraham set out to find a city "whose architect and builder" was God (Hebrews 11:8-10). John saw it descending from heaven to earth. God, as architect and builder, has unlimited resources to complete it. It is the Jesus prepared city. We are even now its citizens. He will bring it down in that glorious day when heaven and earth will finally be one. We can't even imagine our future made possible by our Lord's triumph over death.

"Then I saw a new heaven and a new earth; for the first heaven and the first earth had passed away, and the sea was no more. And I saw the holy city, the new

Jerusalem, coming down out of heaven from God, prepared as a bride adorned for her husband. And I heard a loud voice from the throne saying, "See, the home of God is among mortals. He will dwell with them; they will be his peoples, and God himself will be with them; he will wipe every tear from their eyes. Death will be no more; mourning and crying and pain will be no more, for the first things have passed away." Revelation 21:1-4 (NRSV)

5-19
Trust

Someone said, "I would rather walk with God in the dark than to walk alone in the light." It is safer with God in the battle than without Him on a peaceful beach. It is so much better to trust Him than to be left to trusting our own devices. He who made a path in the wilderness for Israel has given us Jesus as our Path. He is more than a guide; He is our Companion for the journey. Don't be afraid. Renounce fear! Trust! God is with you!

"Trust in Him at all times, O people; Pour out your heart before Him; God is a refuge for us." Psalms 62:8 (NASB)

5-20
A Good Heart

"Every man's way is right in his own eyes, But the LORD weighs the hearts" (Proverbs 21:2 NASB). We rational beings know how to justify our own behavior.

99

Since our heart has its reasons for its actions then we think it is okay. God knows the heart. His Spirit inside us wants to aid the heart to do the right thing for the right reasons. We desire that the Creator would do a recreative work inside of us so that He can say as at creation, "It is good."

5-21
The Connection

Christian, you are a living branch of the Living Vine. We are in Christ and Christ is in us. We make our home in Him and He makes His home in us. Our connection is mutual and vital. We are dependent on this connection for life and fruit bearing. He graciously shares His Spirit with us. Who He is flows into and out of us. He is our connection to the Father. Apart from Him we can do nothing. In Him, we have His inner strength for living and mission.

"Abide in Me, and I in you. As the branch cannot bear fruit of itself unless it abides in the vine, so neither can you unless you abide in Me. I am the vine, you are the branches; he who abides in Me and I in him, he bears much fruit, for apart from Me you can do nothing." John 15:4-5 (NASB)

5-22
Workers With God

Dr. Timothy Green reminds us that, "God is not a micro manager." God gives us freedom to be co-laborers together with Him in His world. He partners with us in our sanctification as well as His mission. The *labor* is to be undertaken by His directives and under His management. It is astounding what you and God can do together. It is amazing at the changes it will make in us when we sync our lives with His.

"We then, as workers together with Him also plead with you not to receive the grace of God in vain." 2 Corinthians 6:1 (NKJV)

5-23
Control

It is as essential to spiritual health for a controller to recover from controlling as it is for an addict to recover from addictions. Both are compulsive and both are unhealthy. Controllers like their own authority. They seize or manipulate to get it. It is given to them by others who won't fight it. It is a negative for the person and the community. Jesus is our model in how we properly relate to others. He gave us humble servanthood as the option to control.

"The kings of the Gentiles lord it over them; and those who have authority over them are called 'Benefactors.' But it is not this way with you, but the one who is the greatest among you must become like the youngest, and the leader like the servant. For who is greater, the one who reclines at the table or the one who serves? Is it not the one who reclines at the table? But I am among you as the one who serves." Luke 22:25-27 (NASB)

5-24
Inner Victory

The atonement of Messiah includes cross, tomb and resurrection. He laid down his life for us, entered into death; became out victor over death, sin and demonic powers, evidenced by resurrection. This greatest victory of all history becomes personal when the triumphant Messiah King moves inside of us to defeat all sin, dead things and dark-side things in our hearts. Free on, oh Messiah, free on! Purify your temple! May your light on the altar never go out!

"Thanks be to God, who gives us the victory through our Lord Jesus Messiah." 1 Corinthians 15:57

5-25
Looking Down on Others

Nazareth was known as a *no good* place! This did not condition its citizens to be accepting. This *no good* place looked at Jesus as *no good*. People at the bottom often try to find others they can look down on. Criticism is so self-deceptive, creating an illusion of righteousness. It is also self-descriptive. Criticism tells more about us than the persons we are putting down. It makes wrong people feel right. Yet it is never holy or right.

"Is not this the carpenter, the son of Mary, and brother of James and Joses and Judas and Simon? Are not His sisters here with us?" And they took offense at Him. Mark 6:3 (NASB)

5-26
Jubilee

Deliverance for Israel was the Passover. Deliverance for believers is the historical event of Jesus death, burial, and resurrection. He defeated our enemies to break the bonds of our slavery. By His Spirit, He has come to live in us as Messiah and Lord. Believers attach themselves to the Messiah and His kingdom rule in their lives. We enter a relationship where deliverance, forgiveness and the freedom of jubilee becomes reality.

"THE SPIRIT OF THE LORD IS UPON ME, BECAUSE HE ANOINTED ME TO PREACH THE GOSPEL TO THE POOR. HE HAS SENT ME TO PROCLAIM RELEASE TO THE CAPTIVES, AND RECOVERY OF SIGHT TO THE BLIND, TO SET FREE THOSE WHO ARE OPPRESSED, TO PROCLAIM THE FAVORABLE YEAR OF THE LORD." *(i.e. Jubilee)* And He closed the book, gave it back to the attendant and sat down; and the eyes of all in the synagogue were fixed on Him. And He began to say to them, "Today this Scripture has been fulfilled in your hearing." Luke 4:18-21 (NASB)

5-27
Bright Path

Jesus is the path we travel. His teachings are the high road! His footsteps will not lead us astray. You will see other travelers on other roads. They will try to lure you to their winding trail. All ways don't lead home. One does. He, The Ancient of Days, is the

Ancient path of Jeremiah. He is the Highway of Holiness that Isaiah saw leading the people out of Exile. His way "shines brighter and brighter until the full day" (Proverbs 4:18).

Thus says the LORD, "Stand by the ways and see and ask for the ancient paths, Where the good way is, and walk in it; And you will find rest for your souls. But they said, 'We will not walk in it.' Jeremiah 6:16 (NASB)

5-28
The Gift of Presence

One of the greatest gifts you can give another person is to be present with them. To be there for them! Listening! Encouraging! Enfolding! Jesus Himself gives us the gift of Presence. No one will ever be more attentive and attuned to what you are saying and where you are than the Ever-Present-One. Give back to Him the gift of presence. Be with Him where He is and discover Him in all your places. Lord, help me to be truly present with you!

"If anyone serves Me, he must follow Me; and where I am, there My servant will be also; if anyone serves Me, the Father will honor him" (John 12:26 NASB). "Father, I desire that they also, whom You have given Me, be with Me where I am, so that they may see My glory which You have given Me, for You loved Me before the foundation of the world" (John 17:24 NASB)

5-29
Made to Worship

We are made to honor and worship something beyond ourselves. It is the way the universe works. Everything exists to complement, enhance and to be a part of something else. Even the Trinity exists in a community of mutual self-giving agape love. Failure to worship is to deny your essential self the glory of becoming what you were meant to be. You and those you love will be increasingly changed by worship.

"Praise the Lord! Praise God in His sanctuary; Praise Him in His mighty expanse. Praise Him for His mighty deeds; Praise Him according to His excellent greatness." Psalm 150:1-2 (NASB)

5-30
Truth and Freedom

Jesus said, "You will know the truth, and the truth will make you free" (John 8:32). We want truth shaped by national consensus. We want truth based on opinion polls. Truth sits above all of that and is the judge of all of our opinions. Truth and wisdom flow from God as its source. Truth is not democratic. We don't vote it in and we don't vote it out. Where truth does not reign, freedom dies.

5-31
Our Messiah Will Judge Us

Is there any thought more sobering than, "We shall all appear before the judgment seat of Christ to give account of our deeds?" Our works and our deeds matter enough to God that, in the end, He will judge us based on these actions. Why so? Because our deeds flow from the person we have become. When we are right with God and the persons around us, righteous deeds flow naturally.

"Therefore we also have as our ambition, whether at home or absent, to be pleasing to Him. For we must all appear before the judgment seat of Christ, so that each one may be recompensed for his deeds in the body, according to what he has done, whether good or bad." 2 Corinthians 5:9-10 (NASB)

6-1
Path-Way

Jesus is the Path we walk and the Light which shines on the path. He came from the Father and is our Way to the Father. To live His teachings is the way we walk the Way. His way is truth and it leads to life. Living our way through life leaves us empty and floundering for direction. He is the Way through our wilderness. Walking this Path matures us as we journey to the Father's house.

"Jesus said* to him, "I am the way, and the truth, and the life; no one comes to the Father but through Me." John 14:6 (NASB)

6-2
Obedience And Knowing

Willingness to do God's will opens the way to knowing God's will. Knowing begins in humble obedience to God. Breaking His commandments produces the blindness of *not knowing*. Obedience unfolds God's plan for you. Jesus said, 'My teaching is not Mine, but His who sent Me. If anyone is willing to do His will, he will know of the teaching, whether it is of God or whether I speak from Myself' (John 7:16-17 NASB).

6-3
Words of Eternal Life

Jesus said to the twelve, "You do not want to go away also, do you?" Simon Peter answered Him, "Lord, to whom shall we go? You have words of eternal life" (John 6:67-68 NASB). The teachings of Jesus are the words that guide our lives. We are to relish these sayings, meditate on them and put them into practice, until they become who we are. His way of living life and relating to people is unsurpassed. Where would we be without the teachings of Jesus?

6-4
Follow Your Leader

Jesus Messiah is your much needed Guide for the journey. Don't leave home without Him. Keep your Guide in front of you. Follow Him. Don't try to run past Him. Don't lag behind when He is on the move. He knows you better than you know yourself. He knows what to lead you through so that you can become who He wants you to be. This is not a tour you are on. It is conquest. He is reclaiming you and His creation.

"He who loves his life loses it, and he who hates his life in this world will keep it to life eternal. If anyone serves Me, he must follow Me; and where I am, there My servant will be also; if anyone serves Me, the Father will honor him." John 12:25-26 (NASB)

6-5
Being With Him

"Father, I desire that they also, whom You have given Me, be with Me where I am, so that they may see My glory which You have given Me" (John 17:24, NASB). Our Lord wants to be with us. In being with Him we see His radiant glory. In His presence we are cleansed and renewed to be like Him. Set free! Your service for Him becomes a joy! You will begin to lose your appetite for some things as your appetite for Him increases. When we want to be with Him a fraction as much as He wants to be with us, things will begin to change in our lives.

6-6
Messiah in You

The Lord wants to show up at your work place today. He wants to go with you to work and play. The promised Messiah is in you. You are the incarnation of His Presence in your world. Live as one who is carrying around the Holy One on the inside. Not with a false piety that makes you the center, but as one whose living points to the Center. Let Him live His life through your thoughts, words and actions. Let the Messiah in you touch your world.

"To whom God willed to make known what is the riches of the glory of this mystery among the Gentiles, which is Messiah in you, the hope of glory. We proclaim Him, admonishing every man and teaching every man with all wisdom, so that we may present every man complete in Messiah. For this purpose also I labor, striving according to His power, which mightily works within me." Colossians 1:27-29 (NASB)

6-7
Be Encouraged

Paul said, "We do not lose heart, but though our outer man is decaying, yet our inner man is being renewed day by day." Our present bodies are moving toward decay. It is seen in health issues, waning strength and failing memories. Yet, we have an inner person that can increase in health and maturity as it worships God. God's grace preserves the spirit of His children. His holy ones will not suffer final decay. Someday incorruptible spirits will be joined to incorruptible bodies in the *great resurrection*.

"Therefore we do not lose heart, but though our outer man is decaying, yet our inner man is being renewed day by day. For momentary, light affliction is producing for us an eternal weight of glory far beyond all comparison, while we look not at the things which are seen, but at the things which are not seen; for the things which are seen are temporal, but the things which are not seen are eternal." 2 Corinthians 4:16-18 (NASB)

6-8
It is the Lord's Battle

God is our Shield and Defender. He is our Strong Tower and Fortress. He does not exempt His children from life's struggles and troubles. However, He is vigilant in protecting us from the traps of our enemy. He knows where the arrows come from, and is trying to prepare us before the enemy even pulls the bow string. Dwell with Him. He is the safe place. Do not fear. God is with you.

"He shall say to them, 'Hear, O Israel, you are approaching the battle against your enemies today. Do not be fainthearted. Do not be afraid, or panic, or tremble before them, for the Lord your God is the one who goes with you, to fight for you against your enemies, to save you'." Deuteronomy 20:3-4 (NASB)

6-9
The Inside Matters

All spirituality begins in the heart and flows out. The outward is rooted in the inward. Acts of righteousness should be driven by true compassion in the soul. Holiness is driven by loving God with an undivided heart. The intent and motive of the heart matters. He who calls us, calls us to be pure in heart. He enables what He commands.

"Almighty God, unto whom all hearts be open, all desires, known, and from whom no secrets are hid: cleanse the thoughts of our hearts by the inspiration of the Holy Spirit, that we may perfectly love thee, and worthily magnify thy holy name, Through Jesus Christ our Lord, Amen." (From the Book of Common Prayer)

6-10
Trusting

God is with us. When we can't see Him, He sees us. When we can't feel Him, His heart is moved toward us. He knows what He is seeking to accomplish in our lives even when we are asking, "Why"? We live in the assurance that He is God and is doing something in our lives beyond our present comprehension. Our task is not to figure out everything but to trust and obey in all things.

"Behold, I go forward but He is not there, And backward, but I cannot perceive Him; When He acts on the left, I cannot behold Him; He turns on the right, I cannot see Him. But He knows the way I take; When He has tried me, I shall come forth as gold." Job 23:8-10 (NASB)

6-11
Listen to Wisdom

Jesus Christ is the Wisdom that causes life to make sense. He is the Wisdom that was with God before creation and He is God. Wisdom was incarnate in Jesus. He is the "true knowledge of God's mystery, that is, Christ Himself, in whom are hidden all the treasures of wisdom and knowledge" (Colossians 2:2b). Ask wisdom of Wisdom's Source. Attentiveness to His inner voice can give insight into all of our problems.

"But if any of you lacks wisdom, let him ask of God, who gives to all generously and without reproach, and it will be given to him. But he must ask in faith without any doubting, for the one who doubts is like the surf of the sea, driven and tossed by the wind." James 1:5-6 (NASB)

6-12
God Cares

The size and expanse of the universe is beyond our ability to comprehend. The creation declares the greatness of the Creator. Humans are mere cosmic dust compared to all that is out there. But, the revelation of Scripture is that God thinks about us and cares for us. He cares so much that He sent His one and only Son to rescue us. Lift up your head. God cares for you more than you can comprehend.

"When I consider Your heavens, the work of Your fingers, The moon and the stars, which You have ordained; What is man that You take thought of him, And the son of man that You care for him?" Psalm 8:3-4 (NASB)

6-13
Face it with the Lord

Just to think about facing or dealing with some things can be unsettling. We may feel fear, inadequacy, or even panic. If we focus on the problem too much, it ceases to be problem solving. The problem starts shaking us around. Face it with the Lord and He can de-fear the situation. "The Lord is my light and my salvation; Whom shall I fear? The Lord is the defense of my life; Whom shall I dread?" Psalm 27:1 (NASB).

6-14
Embracing the Suffering Servant

Saint Paul wrote, "That I may know Him and the power of His resurrection and the fellowship of His sufferings, being conformed to His death" (Philippians 3:10 NASB). There is a deeper knowledge of Jesus Christ that only comes through times of suffering. In these times of suffering we identify with Him and know that He identifies with us. We think about the things He went through and allow the Holy Spirit to apply the parallel. We embrace the Suffering Servant and He embraces us. It is a knowing embrace.

6-15
Feeling with Another

"Rejoice with those who rejoice, and weep with those who weep," is a directive of the Apostle Paul (Romans 12:15). We tend to be focused on our own rejoicing and weeping and never experience the emotions of those around us. This directive calls us to experience incarnational empathy and oneness with our fellow humans. It changes both of us. It keeps me from being selfish and encourages the recipient. It bonds the Father's children.

6-16
A Bargain

Jesus asks us to lose our life so that we might find it. He asks us to die so that we might live. He asks us to deny our self to free us from selfishness. He gives us more back than we can ever give Him. He gives us back our true self. He gives us back our very lives. We begin to live in a way we could not have dreamed.

"For whoever wishes to save his life will lose it; but whoever loses his life for My sake will find it." Matthew 16:25 (NASB)

6-17
The Workings of Grace

God sometimes, as an act of grace, permits us to lose things we do not want to part with. We may cry as a child who has lost her doll. Yet in the process of being stripped of something we hold dear, we find a deeper union with the One of ultimate worth. We would not want to repeat the experience, but know that we are better because of it. More mature! Refined by fire! Oh the surprising gifts of grace! Be grateful!

Then Job arose and tore his robe and shaved his head, and he fell to the ground and worshiped. He said, "Naked I came from my mother's womb, And naked I shall return there. The Lord gave and the Lord has taken away. Blessed be the name of the Lord." Through all this Job did not sin nor did he blame God. Job 1:20-22 (NASB)

6-18
Shalom

Shalom is the great Hebrew word for peace. It is a word that speaks of more than the absence of war. Shalom means *well being, wholeness* or *completeness.* It is something individuals and communities experience. It is health and wholeness in our very being that comes from right relationship to God, to each other, to one's self and to creation. Jesus came to bring this kind of shalom. Peace to you this day, my friend.

Then the Lord spoke to Moses, saying, "Speak to Aaron and to his sons, saying, 'Thus you shall bless the sons of Israel. You shall say to them: The Lord bless you, and keep you; The Lord make His face shine on you, And be gracious to you; The Lord lift up

His countenance on you, And give you peace (*Shalom*).' Numbers 6:22-26 (NASB)

6-19
Our Grace Need

We have inside of us a need for unconditional acceptance even when our behavior may have created barriers with other people. We all have value and worth, no matter what we have done. For someone to reach out to us with grace has a way of calling forth the best that God has placed within us. Grace is an invitation to be better. Grace has a healing touch about it. Someone you know needs grace today.

"For the grace of God has appeared, bringing salvation to all men, instructing us to deny ungodliness and worldly desires and to live sensibly, righteously and godly in the present age" Titus 2:11-12 (NASB)

6-20
Givers of Grace

To give grace is to be a coworker with God. God is a giver of grace and He invites us to join Him in this righteous cause. God gives love, mercy, and forgiveness. All these we receive from Him as acts of grace. All of these we give away as His ambassadors. The Spirit of God is active in grace. Giving grace opens doors for God's loving embrace.

"The God of peace will soon crush Satan under your feet. The grace of our Lord Jesus be with you." Romans 16:20 (NASB)

6-21
God's Co-worker

"For we are God's fellow workers" I Corinthians 3:9a (NASB). Amazing that we can be a coworker with the Creator! We work alongside God, but always under His supervision. Listen to His Spirit as He sets the agenda. Work using His methods and not expecting Him to bless yours. It is pay enough just to work with Him, plus the joy of the apprenticeship. Lord, what do you have for me to do today?

6-22
The Person You Are Becoming

Live by grace toward the person you and God want you to become. Someday you will be your final offering to God (2 Timothy 4:6). May your offering bring glory to Him and joy to you. May it not bring sadness to Him and shame to you. Live your life toward holy character. Be someone who has learned the joy of loving and serving others with a pure heart.

6-23
Complete in Him

You need God. He is the North Star without which you are lost. He is the Keystone without which the arch cannot be erected. He is the Solid-Rock foundation for your life. Without Him, you live with an empty void. Nothing can take His place in your heart. You can shove other things into His space, but it will not work. When you know Him as He is, you will find yourself. You are complete in Him because you were meant for Him.

"For in Him all the fullness of Deity dwells in bodily form, and in Him you have been made complete, and He is the head over all rule and authority." Colossians 2:9-10 (NASB)

6-24
Advance Decisions

Some decisions are made in life based on the information we have at the moment. Our primary decisions should be made in advance. Decisions like: God is first in my life; I will live in moral purity; I choose ethical uprightness and honesty; I will avoid addictive substances; I will only choose a true Christian as a soul mate; I will be kind and compassionate to other people. These great decisions keep my daily decisions from running amok.

"But Daniel made up his mind that he would not defile himself with the king's choice food or with the wine which he drank; so he sought permission from the commander of the officials that he might not defile himself." Daniel 1:8 (NASB)

6-25
Praying with the Intercessor

The Son and the Spirit intercede for us before the Father. They always pray for us according to the will of God (Romans 8:26-27, 34). The highest form of prayer is to pray with the Intercessor. When we pray the same thing the Intercessor prays, prayers will be answered. Get in tune with the Spirit in your praying. He will teach you to pray the will of God. Pray with Him.

"This is the confidence which we have before Him, that, if we ask anything according to His will, He hears us. And if we know that He hears us in whatever we ask, we know that we have the requests which we have asked from Him." 1 John 5:14-15 (NASB)

6-26
Hope in Suffering

There is much suffering in this present time. We get through it with God's present sustaining grace and knowing that suffering does not have the final word. The final word is the coming glory that we will experience when He comes. Presently, we may endure pain. But life can be good even in the midst of our difficulties. Hope does not allow suffering to crush us.

"For I consider that the sufferings of this present time are not worthy to be compared with the glory that is to be revealed to us. For in hope we have been saved, but hope that is seen is not hope; for who hopes for what he already sees? But if we hope for what we do not see, with perseverance we wait eagerly for it." Romans 8:18, 24-25 (NASB)

6-27
The Earth

Father we thank you for the beautiful earth in which Your creatures dwell. Forgive us for taking this gift for granted. Forgive us for the way we trash what You have made. You made us stewards of the earth. It is Yours and not ours. You will come in judgment "to destroy those who destroy the earth" (Revelation 11:18). May we amend our ways through repentance to restore and replenish as You commanded us. In the name of the creating incarnate Word, we pray.

"The earth is the LORD's, and everything in it, the world, and all who live in it." Psalms 24:1 (NIV)

6-28
Peace with God

"Therefore, having been justified by faith, we have peace with God through our Lord Jesus Christ" Romans 5:1 (NASB). What a gift to be at peace with God! Hostilities gone! Reconciliation accomplished! Grace received! All based on a relationship of faith and confidence; not on the law and fear. If we make God our enemy, it is all on our part. His heart beats to be near us. In Jesus, the Father welcomes sinners to dine with Him at the table of peace.

6-29
The Peace of God

Peace with God is the door whereby we enter the peace of God. It is to step into a new dimension. Before we had peace with God, other thoughts and fears occupied our hearts and minds. Paul gave some directives that cultivate peace. Rejoice! Be gentle! Know the Lord is near! Avoid anxiety! Pray! Make your requests to God! Thanksgiving! Then the incomprehensible peace of God will hold your inner being steady!

"Rejoice in the Lord always; again I will say, rejoice! Let your gentle spirit be known to all men. The Lord is near. Be anxious for nothing, but in everything by prayer and supplication with thanksgiving let your requests be made known to God. And the peace of God, which surpasses all comprehension, will guard your hearts and your minds in Christ Jesus." Philippians 4:4-7 (NASB)

6-30
Enthroned Peace

Jesus Messiah is the Prince of Peace, Lord of all creation. His rule begins in the community of believers, in their hearts and minds, flowing to all the earth. When Messiah truly rules in me, His peace, shalom (wellbeing and wholeness) begins to grip and reorder my life. His peace enthroned in me becomes a ruling principle that orders my life in ways that are just and right, even through chaos but without becoming chaotic. Blessed inner peace!

"Let the peace of Christ rule in your hearts, to which indeed you were called in one body; and be thankful." Colossians 3:15 (NASB).

7-1
The Path of Peace

Peace is a path we walk and a relationship in which we live. Jesus is the Sun light that shines on the way of peace. "Because of the tender mercy of our God, With which the Sunrise from on high will visit us, TO SHINE UPON THOSE WHO SIT IN DARKNESS AND THE SHADOW OF DEATH, To guide our feet into the way of peace" Luke 1:78-79 (NASB). To walk the Jesus way, obeying His teachings is to know the peace He came to bring.

"They do not know the way of peace, And there is no justice in their tracks; They have made their paths crooked, Whoever treads on them does not know peace." Isaiah 59:8 (NASB)

7-2
Peace and the Spirit

Jesus promised to leave His peace with us. It is not a peace that this world can give. His promise of peace was in the context of giving to His followers the Helper, the Holy Spirit. The Holy Spirit is essential to inner peace. He guides us into the way of peace. It is our Lord whose countenance shines on us to give us peace in the face of what would otherwise cause fear. He teaches us how to be at peace while being peacemakers.

"These things I have spoken to you while abiding with you. But the Helper, the Holy Spirit, whom the Father will send in My name, He will teach you all things, and bring to your remembrance all that I said to you. Peace I leave with you; My peace I give to you; not as the world gives do I give to you. Do not let your heart be troubled, nor let it be fearful." John 14:25-27 (NASB)

7-3
Internal Guidance System

The Passover was a festival that celebrated deliverance from Egypt. Pentecost became a festival that celebrated the giving of the law through Moses. Pentecost fulfilled the prophecy, "I will put My law within them, and on their heart I will write it; and I will be their God, and they shall be My people" Jeremiah 31:33b (NASB). We need an internal guidance system vs. external law. We need God inside of us to guide us in our living and doing.

"Moreover, I will give you a new heart and put a new spirit within you; and I will remove the heart of stone from your flesh and give you a heart of flesh. And I will put My Spirit within you and cause you to walk in My statutes, and you will be careful to observe My ordinances" Ezekiel 36:26-27 (NASB).

7-4
To Himself

God's rescue of His people from Egypt was more than bringing them into Canaan; it was about bringing them to Himself. "You yourselves have seen what I did to the Egyptians, and how I bore you on eagles' wings, and brought you to Myself" Exodus 19:4 (NASB). His walk with you through your wilderness is preparing you for a new more intimate fellowship with the Father. Go through it with Him and you will come out on the other side nearer to Him.

7-5
Mutual Abiding

God wants to make His home in us and wants us to make our home in Him. This is what is meant by abiding. Jesus used the vine and branch to illustrate this. The Spirit of Jesus (i.e. the Holy Spirit) is His dwelling in us. "I in them and You in Me, that they may be perfected in unity...so that the love with which You loved Me may be in them, and I in them" John 17: 23, 26 (NASB). Mystery, but real union! Dwelling with love! Love dwelling in me! Spirit fullness! Precious!

"Abide in Me, and I in you. As the branch cannot bear fruit of itself unless it abides in the vine, so neither can you unless you abide in Me. I am the vine, you are the branches; he who abides in Me and I in him, he bears much fruit, for apart from Me you can do nothing" John 15:4-5 (NASB).

7-6
Soul Thirst

As the body thirsts for water, and must have it to survive, so the inner being has its thirst. Jesus satisfies the thirst of the soul. Some claim Jesus as their ticket to the future but have not discovered the inner satisfaction of Spirit intimacy. He is not a bottle to carry with you, but a spring bubbling up on the inside. The world has its water substitutes that leave us deceived and still thirsty. Jesus is pure water! Drink deeply and fully!

"If anyone is thirsty, let him come to Me and drink. He who believes in Me, as the Scripture said, 'From his innermost being will flow rivers of living water.'" But this He spoke of the Spirit, whom those who believed in Him were to receive; for the Spirit was not yet given, because Jesus was not yet glorified" John 7:37b-39 (NASB).

7-7
Persevere

Sometimes sorrow's road is longer than we expected. The load is heavier! The night is darker! Problems mount up faster than solutions. Don't give up! Persevere! Embrace hope! Let the ancient words of Scripture renew you! "For whatever was written in earlier times was written for our instruction, so that through perseverance and the encouragement of the Scriptures we might have hope" Romans 15:4 (NASB). Every moment, hold on!

7-8
Really Close

God dwelt in the tent to be near His people as they made the Exodus journey. He dwelt in the Temple in the Holy of Holies when they were settled in the land. That was not close enough. He came in the Incarnation as Emmanuel, God with us. That was not close enough. He had something better. On the day of Pentecost He came to dwell in the hearts of His people making them the temple. You can't get closer than that!

"But I tell you the truth, it is to your advantage that I go away; for if I do not go away, the Helper will not come to you; but if I go, I will send Him to you" John 16:7 (NASB).

7-9
Help in Prayer

Both God and Satan come to us at the points of our weaknesses. Satan comes to trap, ensnare and destroy. God's Spirit comes to strengthen, heal and restore. Prayer is one key place God's strength is mediated. Even when we stumble in our words, the Spirit's intercession lifts our prayer to the Father and makes it intelligible. He only takes petitions to the Father for us that are according to God's will. My weakness and stumbling words need the Spirit's help.

"Likewise the Spirit helps us in our weakness; for we do not know how to pray as we ought, but that very Spirit intercedes with sighs too deep for words. And

God, who searches the heart, knows what is the mind of the Spirit, because the Spirit intercedes for the saints according to the will of God" Romans 8:26-27 (NRSV).

7-10
The Spirit of the Way

We often quote Jesus words, "I am the Way, the Truth and the Life." John called the Holy Spirit the *Spirit of Truth*. Paul called Him the *Spirit of life*. Since He is the Spirit of Jesus, He can also be called the *Spirit of the Way*. It is the Spirit inside us that keeps us on the right highway and away from destructive detours. He keeps us focused on Jesus, enabling discernment of truth and error. He speaks Jesus' ways to the inner self. Stay tuned!

"Enter through the narrow gate; for the gate is wide and the way is broad that leads to destruction, and there are many who enter through it. For the gate is small and the way is narrow that leads to life, and there are few who find it" Matthew 7:13-14 (NASB).

7-11
What God Wants

Both prophetic and wisdom literature teach: "To do righteousness and justice is desired by the LORD more than sacrifice" Proverbs 21:3 (NASB).   Our spirituality can fall into a kind of grandiosity of *great* religious experiences and *great* sacrifices because it makes us feel *great*. Real greatness is to set wrongs right! It is to rescue, deliver and restore. It is compassionate action, seeking justice and pursuing mercy. God desires it and still requires it.

"Is this not the fast which I choose, To loosen the bonds of wickedness, To undo the bands of the yoke, And to let the oppressed go free And break every yoke? Is it not to divide your bread with the hungry And bring the homeless poor into the house; When you see the naked, to cover him; And not to hide yourself from your own flesh? Then your light will break out like the dawn, And your recovery will speedily spring forth; And your righteousness will go before you; The glory of the LORD will be your rear guard. Then you will call, and the LORD will answer; You will cry, and He will say, 'Here I am." Isaiah 58:6-9a (NASB) (Also see Malachi 6:6-8)

7-12
Conquered and Free

Messiah won for us on the cross. The victory He won for us needs to be won in us. He wins in us by the work of His Spirit. We surrender to Messiah as Lord and Victor. Conquered by Him makes the captive free. No longer sin's slaves, but Messiah's slave finding glorious freedom. The sacrificial Lamb is the winner. Live your life in solidarity with Him and you can't lose. The great victory parade is arriving! Listen for the trumpet!

"It was for freedom that Messiah set us free; therefore keep standing firm and do not be subject again to a yoke of slavery." Galatians 5:1 (NASB)

7-13
Face It

When Jesus prayed in the garden on the eve of the crucifixion we remember His words, "Not my will but thy will" but we have forgotten His words, "Arise, let us be going." The first statement prepares disciples for the next statement. Having embraced the will of God, we must arise to embrace the cross. We, too, must get up with resolve, go forward and face life the way it is. Jesus showed us how!

"Then He came to His disciples and said to them, "Are you still sleeping and resting? Behold, the hour is at hand, and the Son of Man is being betrayed into the hands of sinners. Rise, let us be going. See, My betrayer is at hand." Matthew 26:45-46 (NKJV)

7-14
Authenticity

We cannot be authentic persons without authentic spirituality. If we are not real where we meet God, we are certainly not real anywhere else. If we are genuine in our pursuit of God, it orients life around a center other than ourselves. Honesty and openness with God is the only way to live and be. If I am sincere and genuine in my conversations and confessions to God, I will discover an un-borrowed identity that does not need to hide or wear a mask.

"Every day they continued to meet together in the temple courts. They broke bread in their homes and ate together with glad and sincere hearts, praising

God and enjoying the favor of all the people." Acts 2:46-47a (NIV)

7-15
Not Knowing

The children of Abraham never know where they are going. However, they do know who has called them and they know who is going with them. The future events of our lives are not ours to know. It is ours to know the Lord, to walk with Him one step at a time. When Abraham was walking with his Friend, in faith and trust, unknown things had a way of working out and becoming God things. Lead On O King Eternal!

"By faith Abraham, when he was called, obeyed by going out to a place which he was to receive for an inheritance; and he went out, not knowing where he was going. By faith he lived as an alien in the land of promise, as in a foreign land, dwelling in tents with Isaac and Jacob, fellow heirs of the same promise." Hebrews 11:8-9 (NASB)

7-16
The First Moments

We give God honor and worship on the first day of the week, The Lord's Day. Find a way to give God the first moments of each day. It may not be as long as you want it to be, but purpose in your heart to begin your day speaking to your Abba and listening for His word to you. "Let me hear Your lovingkindness in the morning; for I trust in You; Teach me the way in which I should walk; for to You I lift up my soul" (Psalm 143:8, NASB).

7-17
Witness of the Spirit

Christian assurance goes beyond a formula to a true inner witness. God has put His Spirit inside the believer, and His Spirit, in our spirit, cries out *"Abba! Father!"* This is the witness of the Spirit, true worship springing up in your spirit to your *Abba! Father!* To have this witness is to be inwardly assured that you are the Father's child.

For you have not received a spirit of slavery leading to fear again, but you have received a spirit of adoption as sons by which we cry out, "Abba! Father!" The Spirit Himself testifies with our spirit that we are children of God. Romans 8:15-16 (NASB)

7-18
Led by the Spirit

One mark of the children of God is that they are led by the Spirit and walk their lives in step with the true Spirit of the Universe, the Spirit of our Lord Jesus Christ. "For all who are being led by the Spirit of God, these are sons of God" Romans 8:14 (NASB). So adjust your pace to the Spirit's pace. May He touch your eyes so you can see what He sees! May He touch your ears so you can hear what He hears! Keep your soul tuned to Him.

7-19
Joy Even in Sorrow

We see and sometimes experience things in life that are sad beyond words. We may shed tears as we bear these pains. Some things could have been prevented, but choices were made that have put events in motion. We live out their sadness. These sadnesses must not be allowed to steal our present joy. God helps us to grow and triumph in the midst of it all with the joy of His abiding presence.

"Then the virgin will rejoice in the dance, And the young men and the old, together, For I will turn their mourning into joy And will comfort them and give them joy for their sorrow." Jeremiah 31:13 (NASB)

7-20
Inner Strength

Without inner strength you can't go on. Someone must help you; indeed someone is ready to help you. When you depend on your reserves of strength, they quickly run out. God gives power for your inner person, the place you need it most. His inner strength is nothing less than filling us with Himself. With Him comes love and grace more than enough for you.

"That He would grant you, according to the riches of His glory, to be strengthened with power through His Spirit in the inner man; so that Christ may dwell in your hearts through faith; and that you, being rooted and grounded in love, and to know the love of Christ which surpasses knowledge, that you may be filled up to all the fullness of God." Ephesians 3:16-17, 19 (NASB)

7-21
Three Groanings

There are three that groan in Romans (8:19-23, 26). The creation groans and suffers child birth pains awaiting new creation. Christians groan in their suffering awaiting a new body even though they have the Spirit. The Spirit groans in intercession for us because of God's full identification with His creatures. Things are not yet like they will be, so we wait for that great day when God will put all things right.

For the anxious longing of the creation waits eagerly for the revealing of the sons of God. For the creation was subjected to futility, not willingly, but because of Him who subjected it, in hope that the creation itself also will be set free from its slavery to corruption into the freedom of the glory of the children of God. For we know that the whole creation groans and suffers the pains of childbirth together until now. And not only this, but also we ourselves, having the first fruits of the Spirit, even we ourselves groan within ourselves, waiting eagerly for our adoption as sons, the redemption of our body. In the same way the Spirit also helps our weakness; for we do not know how to pray as we should, but the Spirit Himself intercedes for us with groanings too deep for words. Romans 8:19-23, 26 (NASB)

7-22
Chosen to be Holy

"Just as He chose us in Christ before the foundation of the world, that we should be Holy and blameless before Him in love" Ephesians 1:4 (NRSV). God called us out to make us holy. We are chosen in and for holiness. Holiness is expressed in an undivided heart, loving God with our whole being. This is our destiny. This is what we were meant to become. God who is holy invites us to be partakers of who He is. The Spirit inside of us accomplishes it. Unresisted grace always moves us toward holiness.

7-23
Reach Out and Down

Jesus has shown us that we are to reach out to folks at the bottom of the socioeconomic ladder—those who have been shunned, neglected and passed-by. The arrogant and self-centered can never be comfortable with the lowly. They feel they deserve better company. We follow a God who went to the lowest not only to associate with them but to be made one with them. Go to the low places and you will find God is already there.

"Be of the same mind toward one another; do not be haughty in mind, but associate with the lowly. Do not be wise in your own estimation." Romans 12:16 (NASB)

7-24
Eating the Bitter

The Passover's annual eating of bitter herbs is the way Israel re-lives the harshness of their ancestors' slavery. Life has a way of putting things on your plate that are quite bitter. In these times you should re-live the bitter sufferings of our Lord for us, and we will "taste and see that the Lord is good" (Psalm 34:8). The Christian God partakes of our bitter suffering, and we of His. In this we mystically taste the sweetness of our God.

"They shall eat the flesh that same night, roasted with fire, and they shall eat it with unleavened bread and bitter herbs." Exodus 12:8 (NASB)

7-25
Seeking Honor

We crave to be respected and accepted by our peers. We will even use our *spirituality* to get it. Pride often wears a *humble* mask. We prefer position over servanthood. If we seek our own honor, then we won't get the honor and commendation of our Lord. Seek the honor that comes from God and then you can truly feel good about yourself.

"How can you believe, when you receive glory from one another and you do not seek the glory that is from the one and only God?" John 5:44 (NASB)

7-26
Your Cross

The empire made the crosses on which early Christians died. Life makes one for us. This dying on a cross is tied to the very events of our daily lives. Our circumstances and the choices of others bring us to die on a painful-personal cross. It would be nice if crosses were more *spiritual* with less gut wrenching *nitty gritty*. Life is not that way. Remember though, new life is what comes out of these deaths.

"If anyone wishes to come after Me, he must deny himself, and take up his cross daily and follow Me." Luke 9:23 (NASB)

7-27
God Revealed

We do not discover God by our own wisdom-search. Pride in our wisdom wants it so. God is in search of us. For the Christian, Christ crucified is God revealed. He is revealed to us as suffering love; the God who entered into solidarity with hurting humans by incarnation. Man did not and could not have *thought up this plan*, but Christ has revealed it. So, by the cross we have come to know God.

Where is the wise man? Where is the scribe? Where is the debater of this age? Has not God made foolish the wisdom of the world? For since in the wisdom of God the world through its wisdom did not come to know God, God was well-pleased through the foolishness of the message preached to save those who believe. For indeed Jews ask for signs and Greeks search for wisdom; but we preach Christ crucified, to Jews a stumbling block and to Gentiles foolishness. 1 Corinthians 1:20-23 (NASB)

7-28
His Plan for You

"Humble yourselves under the mighty hand of God, that He may exalt you at the proper time. Casting all your anxiety on Him, because He cares for you" (I Peter 5:6-7). God's timing is not the same as ours. Our job is to stay humble, pliable and obedient. Let trust in Him drive out anxiety. He knows where you are. God will choose the time and place when you will be lifted up or brought to the place He has chosen.

7-29
We Need to Worship

There is a fine line between our love of leisure and laziness. We all need to rest and to have times without agendas and to-do list. We also need to worship and bring our children up in the worshiping community. The dangers of not doing that are huge in its consequences for our lives and that of our children. We all need the grace that comes through regular corporate worship. All of us need to worship regularly.

"Ascribe to the LORD, O families of the peoples, Ascribe to the LORD glory and strength. Ascribe to the LORD the glory of His name; Bring an offering and come into His courts. Worship the LORD in holy attire; Tremble before Him, all the earth." Psalm 96:7-9 (NASB)

7-30
The Fulfilled Torah

The Law can't fix us. Never could! It can point out what is wrong but it can't change our behavior. This is why reducing Christianity to a new and better moral code is so inadequate. Messiah came to do inside of us what the law could never do. He came to fill us with love (Romans 5:5) which is the fulfillment of the law. He does this through the internal dynamic of "the law of the Spirit of life".

"For the law of the Spirit of life in Christ Jesus has set you free from the law of sin and of death. For what the Law could not do, weak as it was through the flesh, God did: sending His own Son in the likeness of sinful flesh and as an offering for sin, He condemned sin in the flesh, so that the requirement of the Law might be fulfilled in us, who do not walk according to the flesh but according to the Spirit." Romans 8:2-4 (NASB)

7-31
Living with Truth

Paul talks about those who "who suppress the truth in unrighteousness." The essence of wickedness is that it suppresses truth. Truth always wants to spring up. It is a seed bursting out of the soil. It is a spring boiling up from beneath a rock. Life gets really disordered and crazy when we try to let our own behaviors determine truth. Right action welcomes truth and enables us to live in harmony with the grain of the universe.

"For the wrath of God is revealed from heaven against all ungodliness and unrighteousness of men who suppress the truth in unrighteousness, because that which is known about God is evident within them; for God made it evident to them." Romans 1:18-19 (NASB)

8-1
Release It

"Cast your burden upon the Lord and He will sustain you; He will never allow the righteous to be shaken" (Psalm 55:22, NASB). It is easy for us to be anxious about the events of our lives. God truly cares for us. His care for us is more than an attitude; it is His divine and wise actions on our behalf. He wants us to cast our cares upon Him. We need to do the trusting and let God do the fixing. Trust Him enough to release it to Him.

8-2
New

Jesus said, "Behold I make all things new" (Revelation 21:5)
He invites Jew and Gentile into New Covenant.
He invites aliens and strangers into New Israel.

He invites His creatures into new creation.
He promises a new heaven and a new earth.
He gives us a new start in life.
He gives us a new way to live.
He gives us a new and deeper love for others.
Retune to Him and break out in a new song.
He is ready to start something new in you.

8-3
God is Working for You

If God is at work in all things for our good (Romans 8:28), then there is nothing in life that does not have the potential for our betterment. That's hard to believe in the midst of trouble. God causing all things is a bad definition of sovereignty. In a world where demons and devils are at work, and where people are making choices, God is also at work to achieve His purposes in the lives of His children. You can rest in that without fretting.

"And we know that in all things God works for the good of those who love him, who have been called according to his purpose." Romans 8:28 (NIV)

8-4
Our Shepherd

Jesus is the Good Shepherd. He tends His sheep. He finds still waters for us. He anoints us with oil. He overflows our cup. His rod defends us. He protects us from the wolves. His staff rescues us. He prepares a bountiful table for us. But more than this, the Good Shepherd laid down His life for us when we had deliberately wandered away. We can surely love and follow such a Shepherd as that!

"I am the good shepherd; the good shepherd lays down His life for the sheep. He who is a hired hand, and not a shepherd, who is not the owner of the sheep, sees the wolf coming, and leaves the sheep and flees, and the wolf snatches them and scatters them. He flees because he is a hired hand and is not concerned about the sheep. I am the good shepherd, and I know My own and My own know Me, even as the Father knows Me and I know the Father; and I lay down My life for the sheep." John 10:11-15 (NASB)

8-5
Freedom to Choose

God who is all powerful made a world where people are truly free to make choices. He planted two trees to provide the choice. Giving us freedom is risky for God. He sometimes gets rejected, and because He loves us so much it hurts Him. He could have jumped in and fixed everything by taking our choice back, but for the sake of love He would not use His power to coerce. The Father feels good when His children choose His way.

"Act as free men, and do not use your freedom as a covering for evil, but use it as bondslaves of God." 1 Peter 2:16 (NASB)

8-6
Free to do Right

When the human family uses freedom to disobey God's commands, it brings with it consequent bondage and a loss of freedom. The Savior came to set captives free. In Him the chains of human sin are broken to bring us to a new level of freedom. Yet we are faithfully warned (Romans 6) not to use our new freedom to return to sin's slavery, but instead we are now made truly free to serve God by righteous actions.

"It was for freedom that Christ set us free; therefore keep standing firm and do not be subject again to a yoke of slavery." Galatians 5:1 (NASB)

8-7
A New Master

Slaves were bought and sold in the market place. When Christ bids on us we can accept His bid because His love compelled Him to offer the highest price anyone was ever willing to pay for us. Since I am freed by such love, I choose to live the rest of my life as His bond slave. Irony? Paradox? Yes! There is great joy and glorious freedom in being a servant to Jesus and His mission.

"For when you were slaves of sin, you were free in regard to righteousness. Therefore what benefit were you then deriving from the things of which you are now ashamed? For the outcome of those things is death. But now having been freed from sin and enslaved to God, you derive your benefit, resulting in sanctification, and the outcome, eternal life." Romans 6:20-22 (NASB)

8-8
Live Now

Always wishing we were somewhere else, doing something else, or with someone else steals from us being present for the God-gifts of the moment. This attitude never unwraps His gifts and is offensive to the Giver. Look for blessings everywhere, even in your *bad places.* Keep doing what you are supposed to do and loving those around you. Live the moment where you are with joy and gratitude to God who gave it.

"O Lord, You are my God; I will exalt You, I will give thanks to Your name; For You have worked wonders, Plans formed long ago, with perfect faithfulness" Isaiah 25:1. "In everything give thanks; for this is God's will for you in Christ Jesus." 1 Thessalonians 5:18 (NASB)

8-9
Learn Your Lessons

God has a way of making us repeat our lessons when we don't learn them well. Sometimes the lesson is to teach us something deeper the second time around. Sometimes it is because we were multitasking when He was single-tasking. We think lessons are those that only teach us the facts. God's lessons are developing attitudes like patience, longsuffering,

143

perseverance, kindness, gentleness, forbearance, etc. We have a Great Teacher! He is bent on making real disciples.

"Make me know Your ways, O Lord; Teach me Your paths. Lead me in Your truth and teach me, For You are the God of my salvation; For You I wait all the day." Psalm 25:4-5 (NASB)

8-10
Give Him the Stuff

It is possible to live with an unuttered complaint toward God that He is not being fair to us in our circumstances. Some things are just life! What is happening to you is not the important thing, it is what you allow God to make of you in the process. Give Him all the stuff of your life. He knows how to work with it. He who made us out of dust, has been known to make saints out of the poorest of stuff and from the saddest of circumstances.

Trust in the Lord and do good; Dwell in the land and cultivate faithfulness. Delight yourself in the Lord; And He will give you the desires of your heart. Commit your way to the Lord, Trust also in Him, and He will do it. He will bring forth your righteousness as the light And your judgment as the noonday. Rest in the Lord and wait patiently for Him; Do not fret because of him who prospers in his way, Because of the man who carries out wicked schemes. Cease from anger and forsake wrath; Do not fret; it leads only to evildoing. Psalm 37:3-8 (NASB)

8-11
Healing in His Wings

It takes a certain amount of self-knowledge for us to arrive at deeper inner healing. We can't move on until we deal with who we are and what has come to make us this way. Reading may help. Self-examination and counseling may help. But it takes God-power to enable us to heal, and move beyond where we are to where we should be. This involves letting go, surrender and working with the Healer. It takes sitting in the Son-Light.

"But unto you that fear my name shall the Sun of righteousness arise with healing in his wings; and you shall go forth, and grow up as calves of the stall." Malachi 4:2 (KJV)

8-12
Healing Waters

We long for the healing of our inner self. In a deep inner knowing, we long for a divine touch. The healing of the heart is better than the healing of the body. The outer person is perishing but the inner person is being renewed. Ezekiel saw a River that flows from the temple bringing healing (47:12). Jesus promised it to us (John 7:37-39). This healing stream is His Spirit bringing the wholeness we long for. Flow in me, Oh Healing Waters!

"By the river on its bank, on one side and on the other, will grow all kinds of trees for food. Their leaves will not wither and their fruit will not fail. They will bear every month because their water flows from the sanctuary, and their fruit will be for food and their leaves for healing." Ezekiel 47:12 (NASB)

8-13
Prayer Changes Your Day

Father, I am amazed at all the gifts You hide in difficult circumstances. I am overwhelmed with how You show up in the details. I am surprised that You bring joy in the midst of sorrow. Forgive me Father for all the times I complained about *this or that* and for not seeing You at work in *this and that*. You are an amazing and awesome Father, who calls one like me your child. Bad days are good days when we go for a walk with You. Amen!

"Therefore humble yourselves under the mighty hand of God, that He may exalt you at the proper time, casting all your anxiety on Him, because He cares for you" 1 Peter 5:6-7 (NASB)

8-14
Good Medicine

"A joyful heart is good medicine, but a broken spirit dries up the bones." (Proverbs 17:22, NASB). Have you had your medicine today? Have you given it to anyone else? It is okay to push this tonic, because it is not snake oil and it's not a drug. We are to live in joy and spread joy where we go. Our joy can't be concocted. It must spring from our deep faith in God,

146

and an inner knowing that all is well no matter the circumstances.

8-15
Our Destination

"You yourselves have seen what I did to the Egyptians, and how I bore you on eagles' wings, and brought you to Myself" (Exodus 19:4, NASB). God delivered Israel not merely to bring them to a land, but to bring them to Himself. It is true of us. He is the Destination of our journey! He is not bringing you somewhere, but to Someone. When God acts on our behalf, the action is always an invitation to bring us to the embracing arms of our Father.

8-16
Passive or Active Love

In the South we love everybody, sometimes in a *don't-bother-me, leave-me-alone* kind of way. Some of it goes no deeper than congeniality. (I certainly prefer that to *in-your-face get-out-of-my-way*.) Real love is never passive. By its nature, it has to be active. It gives food and water to bad folks. It prays for mean folks. It retaliates with blessings. It carries burdens for strangers. It walks a mile further than anything else.

"If your enemy is hungry, give him food to eat; And if he is thirsty, give him water to drink." Proverbs 25:21 (NASB)

8-17
Hospitality

God told Israel to be kind to the aliens living among them.   (In Hebrew, *alien* can mean: foreigner, immigrant, sojourner, stranger).   Aliens moving in search of food were to receive hospitality and love among God's people, remembering that when Israel went down to Egypt in search of food, they were treated kindly for 400 years by the Pharaohs. We too were aliens, but have been adopted into the Israel of God (Ephesians 2:12-13).   God's people give hospitality as gratitude for having received it.

"He executes justice for the orphan and the widow, and shows His love for the alien by giving him food and clothing. So show your love for the alien, for you were aliens in the land of Egypt." Deuteronomy 10:18-19 (NASB)

8-18
The Great Weaver

God sees the topside of the tapestry He is weaving. I see the bottom side and complain that the threads look tangled, (and) with no discernible design. The Great Weaver just keeps on weaving together all the strings that make up my life and is not deterred by my complaints.   Lord forgive me. I surrender to the unseen order that you are working in and for me. I re-trust you, Oh Great Weaver. Amen!

"It is God who is at work in you, both to will and to work for His good pleasure" Philippians 2:13 (NASB).

8-19
Grumbling vs. Faith

"Do all things without grumbling or disputing; so that you will prove yourselves to be blameless and innocent, children of God" (Philippians 2:14-15a NASB). Have you ever thought of that as demonstrating that you are a child of God? You can't be grumbling to other people about your situation and trusting your Father at the same time. If we have a Father who loves us, is involved in our lives, and is working His careful plan, then grumbling is a non-faith statement.

8-20
Gratitude's Treasure

"Give thanks to Him; bless His name! For the Lord is good" (Psalm 100:4b-5a). There are treasures hidden within God's commands. The treasure hidden in "give thanks" is contentment and happiness. It is to discover the goodness of God in the midst of the meager. It is an invitation to the assuring knowledge that God is enough for the moment I am now living. Gratitude takes the hand of Abba and walks through anything.

8-21
His Story And Our Story

Believers have entered an ancient story. Our story is now a part of the grand story of what God is doing in His world. When I seek to live my life apart from God's story, I have changed how my story could end, as well as those I love. Stay in His story. Let Him live His story in you. It is going to be wonderful when God's story, which is at work in all of us, is finally told. We will all boast in the Lord's story on that great day.

Indeed, of Zion it will be said, "This one and that one were born in her, and the Most High himself will establish her." The Lord will write in the register of the peoples: "This one was born in Zion." Psalm 87:5-6 (NIV)

8-22
Swim To Shore

When Jesus commanded the waves to be still, it was a demonstration that He was the same One who spoke to the Spirit to move over the chaotic waters at creation. Paul was shipwrecked three times, and God never commanded the storm to stop. In one case, God had promised that there would be no loss of life. He can still our storm or He can say, "grab a plank, hold on and paddle to shore".

"Yet now I urge you to keep up your courage, for there will be no loss of life among you, but only of the ship... But we must run aground on a certain island." Acts 27:22 & 26 (NASB)

8-23
The Words We Speak

Words have great power. We remember negative words spoken to us that hurt us deeply and now may haunt us. We remember positive words spoken to us that drive us to achieve and succeed. Words have power to heal a broken spirit and restore a wounded soul. Speaking the right words can change, comfort, and encourage. Invite the Spirit to help you choose your words and to anoint the ones you speak.

Jesus spoke these words to her, "Neither do I condemn you, go and sin no more" John 8:11b (KJV).

8-24
Baal or I AM

Baal was a god that the ancients tried to manipulate to bring prosperity. It was, "Do all the right things and your cattle and grain will multiply." The God of Israel stands in opposite contrast to that. He is the God whose name is *I AM* or *I will be what I will be*. He is the One we cannot command, control or manipulate. He is who He is. He is God and I am not. Love and obey Him. Walk with Him in total trust. He always gets it right.

Then Moses said to God, "Behold, I am going to the sons of Israel, and I will say to them, 'The God of your fathers has sent me to you.' Now they may say to me, 'What is His name?' What shall I say to them?"

14 God said to Moses, "I AM WHO I AM"; and He said, "Thus you shall say to the sons of Israel, 'I AM has sent me to you.' " Exodus 3:13-14 (NASB)

8-25
Staying Online

Prayer is talking to and listening to God. It is telling Him my heart. It is hearing His heart. What we call "devotions" is our commitment to the process and to the God of the process. We should have blocks of time where we do this, but because of the nature of it, it can never be consigned to a block of time. It is our way of life. Paul tells us to never stop praying. Staying tuned brings the joy of finally hearing our Speaking God.

"Rejoice always, pray without ceasing; in everything give thanks; for this is God's will for you in Christ Jesus" I Thessalonians 5:16-18 (NASB).

8-26
Jesus, Your Boat, and The Storm

Having Jesus is the boat with you is no guarantee that you will not go through storms. All people face storms. Since you are going to face storms, just make sure Jesus is in the boat with you. You may have to bail water. You will have to pray and trust. He does not promise, "No storms". But He does promise that if we trust Him, we will have a safe landing. Having Him for the journey is enough. Besides, He is our destination.

When He got into the boat, His disciples followed Him. And behold, there arose a great storm on the sea, so that the boat was being covered with the waves; but Jesus Himself was asleep. And they came to Him and woke Him, saying, "Save us, Lord; we are perishing!" He said to them, "Why are you afraid, you men of little faith?" Then He got up and rebuked the winds and the sea, and it became perfectly calm. Matthew 8:23-26 (NASB)

8-27
The Hand of God

God has His hand upon you. Don't resist His hand. Don't squirm beneath it. Don't seek to be free of it. Submit to its hold on you. Cling to it as it clings to you. Yield to His hand. You can trust it. It will correct you and it will protect you. It will mature you and it will gift you. It is the hand of blessing.

"The Lord bless you, and keep you; The Lord make His face shine on you, And be gracious to you; The Lord lift up His countenance on you, And give you peace" Numbers 6:24-26 (NASB).

8-28
God Speaks

The real God can speak. Idols can't. The god we construct out of our own imagination is a god the way we want Him to be, the one whose message to us we can control, in whose mouth we can put our words.

The God revealed in the Bible is a God who is free to speak to us in amazing ways with surprising words. Surrender to the God revealed in Christ. Let Him be God. Walk with Him and you will hear His words to you.

"Our God is in the heavens; He does whatever He pleases. Their idols are silver and gold, The work of man's hands. They have mouths, but they cannot speak; They have eyes, but they cannot see; They have ears, but they cannot hear; They have noses, but they cannot smell; They have hands, but they cannot feel; They have feet, but they cannot walk; They cannot make a sound with their throat. Those who make them will become like them, Everyone who trusts in them. O Israel, trust in the LORD; He is their help and their shield." Psalms 115:3-9 (NASB)

8-29
True Giving

True giving cannot come from the heart of an unwilling giver. Real giving flows from who we are. God's grace in our lives should move us toward generosity. When we finally realize the magnitude of God's generous grace toward us, we have both a motive and pattern for giving. If giving is causing you pain, think about God's grace and generosity toward you. Be what God is to you and you will be a generous giver.

Jesus reminds us, "Freely you have received, freely give." Matthew 10:8

8-30
Becoming What We Choose

Oscar Wilde said, "I have learned this: it is not what one does that is wrong, but what one becomes as a consequence of it." The actions we do, good or bad, shape our inner self either in positive or negative ways. In a large measure, we are the accumulation of our chosen actions. When we choose to do the teachings of Jesus, it will form us into a person of character built on a solid Rock.

"Therefore everyone who hears these words of Mine and acts on them, may be compared to a wise man who built his house on the rock" Matthew 7:24 (NASB).

8-31
Choosing Gods

By the time of Joshua, Israel had accumulated gods from "Beyond the River" (Ur/Babylon), Egypt, and the "Amorites in whose land you dwell". A choice had to be made. It was to serve these accumulated gods of the culture or to serve the LORD alone. We too accumulate gods from the culture around us or carry gods from previous times. We must name these gods; put them away, fully embracing one LORD without divided loyalty or diluted faith.

"Now, therefore, fear the LORD and serve Him in sincerity and truth; and put away the gods which your fathers served beyond the River and in Egypt, and serve the LORD. If it is disagreeable in your sight to serve the LORD, choose for yourselves today whom you will serve: whether the gods which your fathers served which were beyond the River, or the gods of the Amorites in whose land you are living; but as for me and my house, we will serve the LORD." Joshua 24:14-15 (NASB)

9-1
No Rivals

God wants His people to love Him with an undivided heart. In a world of many gods, folks had to save a piece of their heart for each. The problem with that is, the one true God becomes just one among many. Our culture also has gods aplenty. They want you to give them a piece of your heart. These false gods never deliver what they promise. There is only One God, so love Him with your whole being. You will find real Life when you do.

"Hear, O Israel! The LORD is our God, the LORD is one! You shall love the LORD your God with all your heart and with all your soul and with all your might." Deuteronomy 6:4-5 (NASB)

9-2
Jesus Redefines Idolatry

Jews living in the Roman era could not understand why they were still oppressed when they had given up idols following the Exile. Jesus' preaching claimed that they were still allowing other gods into their lives. He redefined idolatry to be *mammon* (money/material) or anything that competes with God and divides the heart. What we *serve* may indicate the presence of an idol. Oh Father, I want my heart centered on You!

"No one can serve two masters; for either he will hate the one and love the other, or else he will be loyal to the one and despise the other. You cannot serve God and mammon." Matthew 6:24 (NKJV)

9-3
To Be Human

False gods dehumanize us. We become like what we center on. We become false when we worship false gods. The goal of centering our lives on the God revealed in Jesus is to make us fully human. His teachings are the human thing to do. "Love your neighbor! Love and pray for your enemy! Show contempt to no one! Try to work things out with your opponent. Forgive offenders! Actively do good to and for all!" Jesus' life is the perfect model of human. I want to be like Him!

9-4
Celebrate the Good

Some folks live to celebrate the negative. It is the favorite topic of their conversation; the theme always being, "Ain't it awful!" Legalists focus on law breakers. Moralists focus on the immoral. Perfectionists focus on the imperfect. Politicians focus on the sins of their opponents. It is all backdoor self-righteous commendation. Focusing on the bad will poison your spirit. Focus on the good and wholesome and that is what you will become.

"Finally, brethren, whatever things are true, whatever things are noble, whatever things are just, whatever things are pure, whatever things are lovely, whatever things are of good report, if there is any virtue and if there is anything praiseworthy--meditate on these things. The things which you learned and received and heard and saw in me, these do, and the God of peace will be with you." Philippians 4:8-9 (NKJV)

9-5
Receiving Grace

The measure of our spirituality is not how much we can beat ourselves up in the name of repentance. We confess where we have fallen short or sinned and then we gratefully receive grace. Some Christians will not forgive themselves, not allowing grace to do its full healing work in them. For whatever inner reasons, they have a hard time with grace. Who am I to stop God's grace, even for me! Live in the stream of grace, worship and be thankful.

"I do not set aside the grace of God; for if righteousness comes through the law, then Christ died in vain." Galatians 2:21 (NKJV)

9-6
Let God Give

It takes real humility to receive grace. Some folks can give a gift, but don't know how to gratefully receive one. We must repent of our self-sufficiency, reject the arrogance of earning all we get; bow and humbly receive grace. Be thankful for the smallest of His gifts and let none go unnoticed. Humbly receiving grace from our gracious Father blesses Him and corrects our self-sufficiency. We cannot live without gifts of grace.

"God is opposed to the proud, but gives grace to the humble." James 4:6 (ESV)

9-7
The Arms of God

The arms of God are strong arms. They are Everlasting. They deliver us. They defend us. They protect us. They enable us to triumph over our foes. These are the arms of our Father which also embrace us. When He draws you into the arms of His accepting embrace, the things that you thought mattered before, do not matter now. You are comforted and restored. By His Spirit, His arms can make your arms stronger to do what you need to do.

"You have a strong arm; Your hand is mighty, Your right hand is exalted." Psalms 89:13 (NASB)

9-8
Overconfidence

"Therefore let him who thinks he stands take heed that he does not fall" (1 Corinthians 10:12, NASB). Overconfidence in ourselves ensures that we will stumble and fall. Confidence in God and His strength through us ensures success. We always fail when we depend only on ourselves. We can never fail depending on God. "I can do all things through Him who strengthens me" (Philippians 4:13, NASB). Go then in the strength of your strong God!

9-9
Amazing Love and Amazing Grace

Which is more amazing: Amazing Grace or Amazing Love? "Amazing grace, how sweet the sound that saved a wretch like me!" "Amazing love, how can it be that thou my God should die for me!" Both express the same idea of redemption and salvation. Both give us insight into the heart of God from which they flow. Both give sinners hope and promises their deliverance. Christ Himself is Amazing Love and Amazing Grace!

"The grace of the Lord Jesus Christ, and the love of God, and the fellowship of the Holy Spirit, be with you all." (2 Corinthians 13:14, NASB)

9-10
Ambassadors

You have been appointed as a representative and an ambassador for God. Wherever you go, or whatever you do, you must not forget that. You represent Him in a world that may never see Him unless they see Him in you. You are to find those separated from Him and work at reconciliation. You have the joy of bringing people and God together by the words you say and the life you live. Represent Him well.

"Now all these things are from God, who reconciled us to Himself through Christ and gave us the ministry of reconciliation... Therefore, we are ambassadors for Christ." 2 Corinthians 5:18, 20a (NASB)

9-11
God in Christ

God's revelation of Himself produces awe and reverence. When I think about how God is revealed to us in Jesus Christ of Nazareth, I am filled with amazement. God became flesh. One of us! One with us! He made the invisible God visible, approachable, and touchable. Living with us, for us and now in us. His love is overwhelming. His grace is transforming. Think about Him and be grateful.

"God, after He spoke long ago to the fathers in the prophets in many portions and in many ways, in these last days has spoken to us in His Son, whom He appointed heir of all things, through whom also He made the world. And He is the radiance of His glory and the exact representation of His nature, and upholds all things by the word of His power. When He had made purification of sins, He sat down at the right hand of the Majesty on high." Hebrews 1:1-3 (NASB)

9-12
Celebrate the Giver

Too many persons live their lives without gratitude. They are caught up in getting and receiving but not in being grateful. They live to consume, and think they deserve it. They live as if there is no one outside of them or above them to whom they should say, "Thank You". They need to develop a relationship with the Giver of all good. Celebrating the Giver always transforms the receiver into something better.

"What do you have that you did not receive? And if you did receive it, why do you boast as if you had not received it?" 1 Corinthians 4:7b (NASB)

9-13
Community of the Grateful

Father, I want to thank you for the many gifts you have sent into my life. Often these gifts are the very persons you have placed around us. We give to each other what you have given to us, and receive these gifts from our brothers and sisters as Your gifts. Oh Abba, this community of the grateful feels like Your family! Thank You for including us. Amen!

"I will give thanks to You, O Lord my God, with all my heart, And will glorify Your name forever." Psalms 86:12 (NASB)

9-14
Safe in His Will

"Lord willing, I will see you next week," my friend said. He is right. We have no promise of tomorrow nor of the next hour. God teaches us that our plans may not be His plans and our safe places are not necessarily safe. His will is our Safe Place. There is safety in the good will of our good and Holy Father. Christian maturity wills what the Father wills. Rest in His will today and for all of your tomorrows.

Come now, you who say, "Today or tomorrow we will go to such and such a city, and spend a year there and engage in business and make a profit." Yet you do not know what your life will be like tomorrow. You are just a vapor that appears for a little while and then vanishes away. Instead, you ought to say, "If the Lord wills, we will live and also do this or that." But as it is, you boast in your arrogance; all such boasting is evil. Therefore, to one who knows the right thing to do and does not do it, to him it is sin." James 4:13-17 (NASB)

9-15
You and Your Father

No two children have the same relationship with their heavenly Father. All His Children are enfolded in the same love, but because we are all different, the relationship adjusts to the differences. God meets us where we are and walks with us to the place we should be. This walk is unique for each of us. He knows the path you should take. This journey with your Father is a remarkable adventure and precious treasure. Love on your Abba today.

"Blessed be the God and Father of our Lord Jesus Christ, who has blessed us with every spiritual blessing in the heavenly places in Christ." Ephesians 1:3 (NASB)

9-16
Change Your History

The Son of God came the distance to rescue the human race. He took the initiative. He sought you when you did not seek Him. He came in quest of the whole creation and you were included. He wills none to be lost. Don't run from Him, run to Him. He will receive you. Give up your ways. Where have they gotten you? Embrace His ways. He will change the story of your life. He will change your B.C. history to A.D. (The year of our Lord).

"He was in the world, and the world came into being through him; yet the world did not know him. He came to what was his own, and his own people did not accept him. But to all who received him, who believed in his name, he gave power to become children of God, who were born, not of blood or of the will of the flesh or of the will of man, but of God." John 1:10-13 (NRSV)

164

9-17
Outsiders Made Insiders

We came with no hope and He gave us hope. We came to him unclean sinners; and He washed us and called us saints. We came loving ourselves; now we love our neighbors. We were homeless and on the outside; He brought us inside and made us feel welcome. We came to Him as aliens and strangers; He gave us citizenship papers and wrote our names in a book. Through Messiah, all are invited to become children of Abraham.

"But now in Christ Jesus you who formerly were far off have been brought near by the blood of Christ. So then you are no longer strangers and aliens, but you are fellow citizens with the saints, and are of God's household." Ephesians 2:13, 19 (NASB)

9-18
Time is Opportunity

Time is not repeatable. We must make the most of it now. We are to look for opportunities this day to serve others. Our days are made up of moments and seconds. Alertness enables us to seize little moments to do good to others. "Therefore be careful how you walk, not as unwise men but as wise, making the most of your time, because the days are evil" Ephesians 5:15-16 (NASB). Use time wisely, and you can feel good about your day.

9-19
Be an Overcomer

Overcomer promises in The Revelation: They will "eat of the tree of life which is in the Paradise of God", 2:7; "will not be hurt by the second death", 2:11; "will be given authority over the nations", 2:26; "I will give him the morning star", 2:28; "will be clothed in white garments; and I will not erase his name from the book of life, and I will confess his name before My Father and before His angels", 3:5; "I will grant to him to sit down with Me on My throne, as I also overcame and sat down with My Father on His throne", 3:21; "will inherit these things, and I will be his God and he will be My son" 21:7. Lord, by grace, help me to be an overcomer.

9-20
Inner Voice

We speak from that which is at our center. The one meant to occupy the *god seat* in your heart is the Spirit of Messiah. The most difficult thing you have to do in your life is to make sure He alone sits on your heart's throne. Otherwise you are going to get messages from whomever or whatever you have placed there. Your life and the words you speak flow out of whoever is on the *god seat*. Listen to what you are saying.

"The mouth speaks out of that which fills the heart. The good man brings out of his good treasure what is good; and the evil man brings out of his evil treasure what is evil. But I tell you that every careless word that people speak, they shall give an accounting for it in the day of judgment. For by your words you will be justified, and by your words you will be condemned." Matthew 12:34b-37 (NASB)

9-21
A Closer Walk

Our real hope of future glory is Messiah reigning in our inner kingdom now.   It is not a mere legal transaction between you and God but a real relationship of indwelling.   Claiming a personal relationship with God is not the same as having one. Is He real to you? Do you dwell with each other and in each other?   Are you spending time with Him working together with Him on the relationship?   The more He reigns, the closer the walk.

"That is, the mystery which has been hidden from the past ages and generations, but has now been manifested to His saints, to whom God willed to make known what is the riches of the glory of this mystery among the Gentiles, which is Christ in you, the hope of glory." Colossians 1:26-27 (NASB)

9-22
Criticism

Persons who grew up with criticism have to consciously appropriate grace so that they do not become critics. They find flaws in others but suffer from a flaw.   Criticism can rob you of peace, compassion, kindness, humility, gentleness, patience, mercy, and gratitude. Don't allow yourself to become critical of God's servants or His people. Grace can teach you to reject and let go of your previous conditioning and give space to others.

"So, as those who have been chosen of God, holy and beloved, put on a heart of compassion, kindness, humility, gentleness and patience; bearing with one another, and forgiving each other, whoever has a complaint against anyone; just as the Lord forgave you, so also should you. Beyond all these things put on love, which is the perfect bond of unity. Let the peace of Christ rule in your hearts, to which indeed you were called in one body; and be thankful." Colossians 3:12-15 (NASB)

9-23
Perseverance

Stubbornness is not always a commendable quality of character but perseverance is. Both involve strong will decisions. The first, however, is self-oriented and the second is goal oriented. Perseverance is faith holding on to its Lord and His promises. It grips Jesus' word, "He who endures to the end will be saved." It *hits the wall* but keeps running for the prize. It runs toward the finish line and the embrace of its triumphant Captain.

"Do not, therefore, abandon that confidence of yours; it brings a great reward. For you need endurance, so that when you have done the will of God, you may receive what was promised. For yet "in a very little while, the one who is coming will come and will not delay; but my righteous one will live by faith. My soul takes no pleasure in anyone who shrinks back." But we are not among those who shrink back and so are lost, but among those who have faith and so are saved." Hebrews 10:35-39 (NRSV)

9-24
He Knocks

God is secure enough in Himself to not force His way into our lives. His sovereignty does not mean He is the great controller. He has put the handle to the heart door on the inside. He will not kick the door down. He knocks. His voice calls. All do not open to Him. Those who do will find their heart a sanctuary; the entering Light will force out the darkness; the house will receive a makeover; the invited Guest will become Lord of the house and you will be happy about it.

"Behold, I stand at the door and knock. If anyone hears My voice and opens the door, I will come in to him and dine with him, and He with Me." Revelation 3:20 (NKJV)

9-25
God Hears

Our God has ears to hear. God heard the prayers and crying of His people (Exodus 3:7), their groaning (Exodus 6:5), their grumblings (Exodus 16:12), their complaints (Numbers 14:27), etc. He is attentive to our words.   Our words express faith or doubt;

compassion or hostility; grace or judgment. Our words reflect how we are growing in our faith walk. What we say and how we say it matters to God.

"Let the words of my mouth and the meditation of my heart be acceptable in Your sight, O LORD, my strength and my Redeemer." Psalm 19:14 (NKJV)

9-26
Your Wilderness

God loves you and is maturing you through your wilderness. Israel was tested in the wilderness. Jesus was tested in the wilderness. You will be tested there. Expect it. There will be dry and hungry places. There will be times you walk by faith and not feelings or sight. You may feel He is not near, but you follow Him not for the loaves and fish. You are walking with Him because He is God and is bringing you to maturity.

"But He led forth His own people like sheep And guided them in the wilderness like a flock; He led them safely, so that they did not fear; But the sea engulfed their enemies. So He brought them to His holy land, to this hill country which His right hand had gained." Psalm 78:52-54 (NASB)

9-27
Listen and Sing

God is working through the everyday events of our lives to move us to our full and unique potential. He knows where He wants us to be. We compete with the process when we are bent on doing something else. We are pursuing things we want to *do*, while He is pursuing what He wants us to *be*. If this harmony that God has designed for us is going to work, then we need to learn to hear and sing the song like He is writing it.

"Thus says the LORD of hosts, the God of Israel, 'Go and say to the men of Judah and the inhabitants of Jerusalem, "Will you not receive instruction by listening to My words?" declares the LORD." Jeremiah 35:13 (NASB)

9-28
A Life Secret

Some people are motivated by a desire to always be right.
Others are motivated by a desire to always be helpful.
The first group can never be happy.
The second group lives with joy having discovered a life secret.

Everyone helped his neighbor, and said to his brother, "Be of good courage!" Isaiah 41:6 (NKJV)

9-29
Triumph

Jesus faced His temptations assured that, *He was the beloved Son of the Father*. He knew that the Holy Spirit had anointed Him to take on evil and establish the kingdom (Mark 1:9-13). We triumph over our temptations and struggles by knowing that we have a Father who truly loves us and He has given us His Spirit. You, too, can overcome if you know in your heart of hearts that God loves you and dwells in you.

"You are from God, little children, and have overcome them; because greater is He who is in you than he who is in the world." 1 John 4:4 (NASB)

9-30
Anointed to Win

Messiah means *the anointed one*. Jesus was anointed by the Father with the Spirit at His baptism. Christians also are anointed ones. John the Baptist is clear that the anointed one will anoint His followers with the Holy Spirit. They, too, will be empowered for life and ministry. The Kingdom of God is *Anointed subjects* led by the *Anointed King*. The Spirit anoints you to face life's problems; face wrong and make it right; face evil and defeat it.

John the Baptist said, "Someone a lot stronger than me is coming close behind. I don't deserve to squat down and undo his sandals. I've plunged you in the water, he's going to plunge you in the Holy Spirit" Mark 1:7-6 (KNT).

10-1
Testing Follows Filling

The anointed-with-the-Spirit-one (Messiah) was propelled by the Spirit into the wild to confront and be confronted by evil (Mark 1:9-13). Testing follows filling. The devil's plan was to mess up His mission. The Messiah's plan was to expose evil, defeat it and triumph over it. We will be tested to confront evil in all places, even inside ourselves, see it for what it is and defeat it. The kingdom of God has come for this: to expel dark works, all those not done in love.

"But if I cast out demons with the finger of God, surely the kingdom of God has come upon you. When a strong man, fully armed, guards his own palace, his goods are in peace. But when a stronger than he comes upon him and overcomes him, he takes from him all his armor in which he trusted, and divides his spoils." Luke 11:20-22 (NKJV)

10-2
Loved Children

Dysfunctional families fail to affirm, nurture, and give unconditional love. Harshness, abuse, rejection, criticism are substituted. Persons who come out of these families tend to repeat the cycle. Jesus can break the cycle. The good news is that we are affirmed because we are unconditionally loved by our heavenly Father. We are nurtured by the family of God and His indwelling Spirit. Our mission is to spread the love we have received from Him.

"Behold what manner of love the Father bestowed upon us, that we should be called the children of God" I John 3:1b (NASB).

10-3
Live Love

To say, "God loves you" to another, can be trite-- nothing more than a cliché. It may not help. It may hurt. On the other hand if you are filled with the Spirit of love and your eye contact, presence or touch says you truly care, it can be life transforming. If you don't really love them, don't bother to tell them God loves them. Filled-with-love people change others when they live out "God loves you." They rescue hurting scarred people from loveless situations and histories. Go do it! Go be it!

"And so we know and rely on the love God has for us. God is love. Whoever lives in love lives in God, and God in him. We love because He first loved us." 1 John 4:16, 19 (NIV)

10-4
Brokenness

To carry our cross is to live in brokenness, embracing the legitimate pain that flows in and out of our lives. Healthy brokenness does not sound the note of "poor-victim-me". That note destroys the harmony between us and the embrace of the sufferings of Christ. In mystery, we simultaneously experience brokenness and wholeness. This we can't explain but we do experience, bonding to the suffering and triumph of our Lord.

"We are afflicted in every way, but not crushed; perplexed, but not despairing; persecuted, but not forsaken; struck down, but not destroyed; always carrying about in the body the dying of Jesus, so that the life of Jesus also may be manifested in our body. For we who live are constantly being delivered over to death for Jesus' sake, so that the life of Jesus also may be manifested in our mortal flesh." 2 Corinthians 4:8-11 (NASB)

10-5
He Can

Jesus can forgive actions but specializes in fixing hearts. He can take hate out of a heart and replace it with compassion. He can purify a prostitute and make her a part of the bride of Christ. He can change a thief from a taker to a giver. He can free me from me, enabling me to love God and neighbor as I should. He can give strength to the weak, heart to the disheartened and hope to the hopeless. He can! Let him! He will!

"And God is able to make all grace abound to you, so that always having all sufficiency in everything, you may have an abundance for every good deed." 2 Corinthians 9:8 (NASB)

10-6
"In the Right"

When we measure ourselves by moral law, even the Ten Commandments as the means by which we are made right with God, we either condemn or congratulate ourselves! Rather, we are made right with God by trusting Him and the covenant love extended to us through His Son. We live our lives in the inner confident conviction that God is our Father and He loves us. This is how we are made right with God. It is called justification. It is free and freeing. It sets us right with God, others and creation. Morality and ethics, i.e. right behavior, flow out of being rightly related to God.

"The result is this: since we have been declared 'in the right' on the basis of faith, we have peace with God through our Lord Jesus the Messiah. Through him we have been allowed to approach, by faith, into this grace in which we stand; and we celebrate the hope of the glory of God" Romans 5:1-2, (KNT).

10-7
Hate Will Poison

Christians are supposed to love everyone. However today, we have given ourselves permission to hate the other party, the other group, a politician, another team, etc. None of this is innocent and none of it is worthy of followers of Jesus. Hate is always self-destructive. Hate poisons the soul of the hater. Jesus said contempt for another is like murder. When you reserve some compartment of your being for hate, it will infect your soul. Love all!

"You have heard that the ancients were told, 'YOU SHALL NOT COMMIT MURDER' and 'Whoever commits murder shall be liable to the court.' "But I say to you that everyone who is angry with his brother shall be guilty before the court; and whoever says to his brother, 'You good-for-nothing,' shall be guilty before the supreme court; and whoever says, 'You fool,' shall be guilty enough to go into the fiery hell." Matthew 5:21-22 (NASB)

10-8
Jesus' Bedside Manner

Jesus was criticized for eating with sinners and being at their parties. The sin sick were drawn to him. His followers no longer have that *problem*. "*Hate the sin but love the sinner*" frequently comes across to the sinner as hostility and rejection. Our bedside manner does not seem to convey the same compassion as the Galilean Healer. The Great Physician did not drive them away by vibes about their *sickness*. He just loved them and cured them.

When the scribes of the Pharisees saw that he was eating with sinners and tax collectors, they said to his disciples, "Why does he eat with tax collectors and sinners?" When Jesus heard this, he said to them, "Those who are well have no need of a physician, but those who are sick; I have come to call not the righteous but sinners." Mark 2:16-17 (NRSV) "

10-9
The Identifying Mark

When Jesus came, He came as the embodied love of God. The Trinitarian love that He had with the Father from all eternity, He brought into our world. His Spirit filling us is a love filling (Romans 5:5). We, too, embody love when we relate to God and others the way Jesus did. This way, we are in the world like He was in the world. Agape love is the identifying mark that God is living His life in and through us.

"We have come to know and have believed the love which God has for us. God is love, and the one who abides in love abides in God, and God abides in him. By this, love is perfected with us, so that we may have confidence in the day of judgment; because as He is, so also are we in this world." 1 John 4:16-17 (NASB) "

10-10
Your Actual Self

Death to self has often been spoken against as something that destroys personality and personhood. The death to self that Christians talk about is really a death to the sinful or self-centered self. J. O. McClurkan gave this wonderful clarity, "There is a sinful self that needs to die, there is a natural self that needs to be disciplined, there is an actual self that needs to be realized." This heart cleansing and disciplined walk brings freedom to be all you were meant to be.

178

"Then Jesus said to His disciples, 'If anyone wishes to come after Me, he must deny himself, and take up his cross and follow Me. For whoever wishes to save his life will lose it; but whoever loses his life for My sake will find it'." Matthew 16:24-25 (NASB)

10-11
Leaving and Following

The disciples heard Jesus call "Follow me." That call also comes to us. To follow Jesus means to walk away from something. It is to give up anything that prevents you from following. Your old ways of thinking will change. Your values will change. You will walk away from attitudes and reactions that are not like Him. You will have yourself give up all idols as soon as you learn they are idols, so that your life can be truly focused on this follow-Messiah journey.

"After that He went out and noticed a tax collector named Levi sitting in the tax booth, and He said to him, "Follow Me." And he left everything behind, and got up and began to follow Him." Luke 5:27-28 (NASB)

10-12
Remade for Mission

Jesus said, "Follow me, and I will make you...." All humans need a radical reshaping, a recreating. Before the disciples could become fishers of men they had to be reshaped by following Him. Repentance is the way we submit to that ongoing reshaping. The call to be a disciple of Christ means the pursuit of Christlike character and entering His mission. It is a change that thrusts us into our world in all the ways He was in His world.

And Jesus said to them, "Follow Me, and I will make you become fishers of men." Immediately they left their nets and followed Him. Going on a little farther, He saw James the son of Zebedee, and John his brother, who were also in the boat mending the nets. Immediately He called them; and they left their father Zebedee in the boat with the hired servants, and went away to follow Him." Mark 1:17-20 (NASB) "

10-13
Intentionally Follow

Following Jesus is intentional. It is letting His teachings and example guide your life. Humans always follow someone or something. We unthinkingly follow our desires, impulses, the culture, the crowd, money and pleasure. The thing that excites you the most is what you are following. The thing you are most invested in, as seen by time spent, thoughts and conversation is what is leading you. Intentionally follow Jesus. That's what Christians do.

"Many will follow their shameful ways and will bring the way of truth into disrepute." 2 Peter 2:2 (NIV)

10-14
More Than Important

We really do need each other. Believers are an organic part of the body of Christ. Body parts are connected to each other for the health of the whole. We are the family of God. You need the family and the family needs you. Family relationships must be maintained and nurtured. This is really big stuff! More than important! Essential for survival! Plan today and don't let anything keep you away from "body" and "family" tomorrow.

"So let's do it—full of belief, confident that we're presentable inside and out. Let's keep a firm grip on the promises that keep us going. He always keeps His word. Let's see how inventive we can be in encouraging love and helping out, not avoiding worshiping together as some do but spurring each other on, especially as we see the big Day approaching." Hebrews 10:22-25 (The Message)

10-15
"Faith Works by Love"

"Believe in the Lord Jesus Christ and you shall be saved." We do not believe in the biblical sense of the Word without eventually coming to love. "Faith works by love" (Galatians 5:6). The sum of true faith, according to Jesus, is to love God with our whole being and our neighbors as ourselves. Our first response to grace may be out of fear, but we move beyond that to a loving trust. Faith is love trusting. If we truly love Him we will fully trust Him.

10-16
The Alive Word

The most difficult scripture to understand is the most familiar. The way our brain works, we already have the final interpretation filed under *beliefs* where meaning is well established. It's nearly impossible to see or hear something else. God's Word is a Hubble telescope through which to look and we have chosen a peep hole. It is "the living and enduring Word of God" (I Peter 1:23). Dynamic! Not static! Alive! Life transforming! Hear the Spirit of the Word!

"It is the Spirit who gives life; the flesh profits nothing; the words that I have spoken to you are spirit and are life" John 6:63 (NASB).

10-17
Your Burdens

We have to carry our own back pack. We are to help each other with the heavier burdens. The crushing things must be turned over to the Lord. Let God do your heavy lifting. When we finally learn to handle our burdens like Jesus taught us, we find that "His yoke is easy and his burden is light." The load we choose for ourselves kills us. It is unhealthy-crazy to carry your burden to get sympathy; then a sick self is added to the weight. There is peace in releasing it!

"Bear one another's burdens (Greek, one you shouldn't carry alone), and thereby fulfill the law of Christ...For each one will bear his own load (Greek normal individual load) Galatians 6:2, 5 (NASB).

"Cast your burden upon the LORD and He will sustain you" Psalms 55:22b (NASB).

10-18
Prideful or Humble

Prideful people want a high position, so that others can serve them; wealth and power can flow toward them. To imitate this is devilish because that's what Satan did and continues to do. He finds joy in this; it is evil and debauchery. Humble people want a low position, so that they can serve others; wealth and power flows away from them toward human need. To imitate this is divine because that's what Christ did and continues to do. Finding joy in this is righteousness and holiness.

"But He gives a greater grace. Therefore it says, "GOD IS OPPOSED TO THE PROUD, BUT GIVES GRACE TO THE HUMBLE." ...Humble yourselves in the presence of the Lord, and He will exalt you." James 4:6, 10 (NASB)

10-19
Our Gift to Messiah

When we come to Messiah initially, it may be out of self-interest. We are lost! We need rescuing! We need deliverance! He comes to us, the dead, and He raises us to life (Ephesians 2:1-6). Once He delivers us and gives us new life, then love compels us to give that life back to God. Our new motive is to present ourselves as a gift to our Messiah and not to our old sinful master. Romans 6:1-23 calls this sanctification. Give and keep giving yourself to Him who gave Himself to you.

"Do not go on presenting the members of your body to sin as instruments of unrighteousness; but present yourselves to God as those alive from the dead, and your members as instruments of righteousness to God...resulting in sanctification...and the outcome, eternal life. For the wages of sin is death, but the gift of God is eternal life in Christ Jesus our Lord." Romans 6:13, 19, 22-23 (NASB)

10-20
Sword Swinging

When someone comes after you with a sword and a club, it is an easy reaction to return swinging your sword and club. If they come to you with anger, a curse, harshness, etc., the natural reaction is to give it back to them just like they give it to you. Sword and club swinging are not the Jesus way, as we have seen in the frustration of His disciples. His counter intuitive way is to "Put your sword up," give back good for evil and blessings for curses. It is the Jesus way to respond.

"A large crowd with swords and clubs...came and laid hands on Jesus and seized Him. And behold, one of those who were with Jesus reached and drew out his sword, and struck the slave of the high priest and cut off his ear. Then Jesus *said to him, "Put your sword back into its place; for all those who take up the sword shall perish by the sword. Or do you think that I cannot appeal to My Father, and He will at once put at My disposal more than twelve legions of angels?" Matthew 26:47a, 50b-53 (NASB)

10-21
Getting Free From Your History

We are not bound by the history of our situations, individually or as a group! Influenced by it? Yes! Our context? Yes! Bound by it? No! We can be paralyzed because we do not have imagination and appropriated grace to move beyond our histories to a new day. God can take all the things of your history and make it a platform for a new future. But, you have to leave some junk on the trash heap of history and get going with Jesus into your new day.

"At the end of three days the officers went through the camp and commanded the people, "When you see the ark of the covenant of the LORD your God being carried by the levitical priests, then you shall set out from your place. Follow it, so that you may know the way you should go, for you have not passed this way before...Then Joshua said to the people, "Sanctify yourselves; for tomorrow the LORD will do wonders among you." Joshua 3:2-3, 5 (NRSV)

10-22
Transcending Pain

We all live our lives by the way we respond to our pain. Living a life that transcends our deep hurts allows us to be fully embraced by the genuine love and grace of our Messiah. This brings us to a place of maturity where we can even thank God for the pain that is maturing us in His love. By embracing grace, we can express real worship and thanksgiving in the midst of our pain.

"But I am lowly and in pain; let your salvation, O God, protect me. I will praise the name of God with a song; I will magnify him with thanksgiving." Psalms 69:29-30 (NRSV)

10-23
Unacknowledged Blessings

Some gifts in our lives are not seen as gifts until we stop and look at them with thankful eyes. These gifts are indeed blessings, but they do not fully bless because, for whatever reason, we are too distracted to acknowledge them. Father, forgive me for having eyes and not seeing your blessings. Lord, give me eyes to see and a grateful heart so that I do not miss all you are lavishing on me every moment. In the name of Jesus, the Gift. Amen!

"Devote yourselves to prayer, keeping alert in it with an attitude of thanksgiving;" Colossians 4:2 (NASB)

10-24
Hearing the Voice

It takes a trained ear to hear the voice of God. The shepherd David heard it in creation. In our virtual reality world we are no longer present with the created world so we and our children miss it. Eli had to train Samuel's ear to hear it. It whispered to Elijah in a cave. It is perceived in truth. It is imitated in lies. It is overheard in acts of love. It cries to us in the face of human suffering. It is discerned by the one "who has ears to hear". We live by the Voice and starve without it.

"He humbled you and let you be hungry, and fed you with manna which you did not know, nor did your fathers know, that He might make you understand that man does not live by bread alone, but man lives by everything that proceeds out of the mouth of the LORD" Deuteronomy 8:3 (NASB).

10-25
The Main Thing

"You shall love the Lord your God with all your heart, and with all your soul, and with all your mind and with all your strength. The second is this, 'You shall love your neighbor as yourself.' There is no other commandment greater than these" Mark 12:30-31 NRSV). This is the condensed message of the Bible and of Jesus' own teachings. This is the main thing! Lord, may I measure all my thoughts, words and actions by this! Amen!

10-26
Love and Faithfulness

The love and faithfulness of God toward us is greater than we can imagine. Remembering it gives us hope in our darkest hours. To think on it incites praise for our awesome Father. "Praise the LORD, all you nations; extol him, all you peoples. For great is His love toward us, and the faithfulness of the LORD endures forever. Praise the LORD" Psalm 117:1-2 (NIV). Think about and celebrate the love and faithfulness of God towards you!

10-27
Pursue Righteousness

The pursuit of wealth is an empty pursuit that empties the pursuer. To seek what is just and right toward our fellow humans, God and creation is called righteousness. It is the better life pursuit. God promises to provide for those who seek it. "He who is generous will be blessed, for he gives some of his food to the poor" Proverbs 22:9 NASB). God will find more ways to bless those who work for the right than we can imagine.

"For the Gentiles eagerly seek all these things; for your heavenly Father knows that you need all these things. But seek first His kingdom and His righteousness, and all these things will be added to you" Matthew 6:32-33 (NASB).

10-28
True Wealth

God had a claim on us Adams before we wrested it from His hands and took charge of our own lives. Let Him exercise His prior claim on you. Believers can come to a place where Jesus is Lord in reality and not merely in name. Relinquish your claim on yourself. Give Him the claim and the deed. He will find gold, silver and precious stones. Though you have nothing, you will possess all things. When He inherits us, we inherit Him!

"So then let no one boast in men. For all things belong to you, whether Paul or Apollos or Cephas or the world or life or death or things present or things to come; all things belong to you, and you belong to Christ; and Christ belongs to God" I Corinthians 3:21-23 (NASB).

10-29
Inner Turbulence

We sometimes mourn the turbulence of our own waters. We are not always aware of unexamined and un-surrendered things that shake our own inner peace are lying just beneath the surface. The Spirit knows what they are and is anxious to remove them. He calls to me to examine my heart and surrender as a co-laborer with Him in the great work of my continuing purification. O Spirit, make me clean and I will be clean.

189

"So let God work his will in you. Yell a loud no to the Devil and watch him scamper. Say a quiet yes to God and he'll be there in no time. Quit dabbling in sin. Purify your inner life. Quit playing the field. Hit bottom, and cry your eyes out. The fun and games are over. Get serious, really serious. Get down on your knees before the Master; it's the only way you'll get on your feet." James 4:7-10 (The Message)

10-30
Chosen Paths

If you set out for greatness, you will be nothing. You will become self-centered and self-focused. You will celebrate all the wrong things. If you aim at humbly pleasing God and serving others you will discover greatness. If you take the self-path it will become the low road. If you take the God-path it will always become the high road. If you take the low seat, your Lord will call to you in His time, "Come up higher my friend."

"When you are invited by someone to a wedding feast, do not take the place of honor, for someone more distinguished than you may have been invited by him, and he who invited you both will come and say to you, 'Give your place to this man,' and then in disgrace you proceed to occupy the last place. But when you are invited, go and recline at the last place, so that when the one who has invited you comes, he may say to you, 'Friend, move up higher'; then you will have honor in the sight of all who are at the table with you. For everyone who exalts himself will be humbled, and he who humbles himself will be exalted." Luke 14:8-11 (NASB)

10-31
Living in Dying

Total consecration is not easy. Dying on a cross is an ugly messy thing. Yet Jesus embraced it for us! Because He did it for me, I will do it for Him. His love held Him to it. Our love for Him holds us to it. What are the benefits? If we share His cross, we can be His disciple. If we share His death, we will also share His resurrection. When we embrace this very personal dying, His life envelops us. Paradox? Yes, but true!

"For if we have become united with Him in the likeness of His death, certainly we shall also be in the likeness of His resurrection." Romans 6:5 (NASB)

11-1
Continue in the Faith

Continue to choose Jesus today. You trusted Him initially; you can trust Him with a deeper trust now. Continue in faith, believing! Believing the gospel, not moved from the hope it gives. Walking with the Man! Follow the Way until the end of the way. Jesus asks, "Will you also go away?" And we say with His disciples, "To whom shall we go, you have the words of eternal life." No going back, only going forward!

"For we now live, if you continue to stand firm in the Lord" 1 Thessalonians 3:8 (NRSV). "Once you were alienated from God and were enemies in your minds because of your evil behavior. But now he has reconciled you by Christ's physical body through death to present you holy in His sight, without blemish and free from accusation-- if you continue in your faith, established and firm, not moved from the hope held out in the gospel" Colossians 1:21-22 (NIV).

11-2
Truly Living

"Moreover the Lord your God will circumcise your heart and the heart of your descendants, to love the Lord your God with all your heart and with all your soul, in order that you may live" (Deuteronomy 30:6 NASB). Loving God is truly living when we love Him with "all of our heart and soul". It is the purpose of life. It is the fulfillment for which we long. Let Him cut away from your heart all that prevents you from loving Him. Enter the fullness of life that is in Him.

"In him you were also circumcised, in the putting off of the sinful nature, not with a circumcision done by the hands of men but with the circumcision done by Christ, having been buried with him in baptism and raised with him through your faith in the power of God, who raised him from the dead" Col 2:11-12 (NIV).

11-3
Marathon Faith Runners

"And all these, having gained approval through their faith, did not receive what was promised, because God had provided something better for us, so that apart from us they would not be made perfect" Hebrews 11:39-40 (NASB). Our faith story is not complete without their faith, and their story is not complete without ours. We are bound together with them in a great universal faith family. Their example bears fruit in our endurance. Run!

"Therefore, since we have so great a cloud of witnesses surrounding us, let us also lay aside every encumbrance and the sin which so easily entangles us, and let us run with endurance the race that is set before us, fixing our eyes on Jesus, the author and perfecter of faith, who for the joy set before Him endured the cross, despising the shame, and has sat down at the right hand of the throne of God." Hebrews 12:1-2 (NASB)

11-4
Meaning It

When I say, "Lord" to my Messiah, I want it to resonate in my heart, soul, and mind. I want it to be the reality of the inner me and not merely the claim of my lips. When I say, "Lord" may I feel both humility and awe. May this word trigger the love chords in the deepest places of who I am! May I hasten to Him as one does a special friend but with the reverence of one who meets his Sovereign King! May my life be built around this true center!

"Flee the evil desires of youth, and pursue righteousness, faith, love and peace, along with those who call on the Lord out of a pure heart" 2 Tim 2:22 (NIV). "Grace to all who love our Lord Jesus Christ with an undying love" Ephesians 6:24 (NIV).

11-5
False Freedoms

Individuals and nations can live under the illusion of enjoying freedom while being the slaves of corruption. These false freedoms may be held to and defended tenaciously. The one who binds wants you to think you are free. He grants a sweet morsel now and then to keep you where you are. Lord, grant us, as your people, eyes to discern and escape false freedoms.

"For speaking out arrogant words of vanity they entice by fleshly desires, by sensuality, those who barely escape from the ones who live in error, promising them freedom while they themselves are slaves of corruption; for by what a man is overcome, by this he is enslaved." 2 Peter 2:18-19 (NASB)

11-6
Cleansing Our Spirit

"Therefore, having these promises, beloved, let us cleanse ourselves from all defilement of flesh and spirit, perfecting holiness in the fear of God" (2

194

Corinthians 7:1 NASB).   Holiness is as comprehensive as setting apart our whole being. We can pride ourselves in not partaking of certain sins of the flesh but have sins of the spirit manifested by attitudes that are just as defiling to the spirit as sexual immorality is to the body.   God's promises call for cleansing of all.

11-7
Cultivate Gratitude

Think of gratitude as a precious plant in your garden that must be cultivated to thrive. Gratitude leads me away from self-focus to remind me that I am constantly showered with seen and unseen gifts from God and people who touch my life. Cultivation means that I try to think of unseen or under acknowledged things and thank God and individuals for these gifts. It lifts my spirit as I see how incredibly blessed I am.

"In God we have boasted continually, and we will give thanks to your name forever." Psalms 44:8 (NRSV)

11-8
Enough Bread

The disciples were worried about not having resources to feed the crowd. After Jesus had fed 9,000 people in two miracle multiplications of bread, the disciples are fretting over no bread in the boat. If the living "Bread come down from heaven" is in the boat with us, it is enough. He is the sufficient Bread that is never diminished by our partaking. We receive and are satisfied and there are always baskets left that we could not contain.

Jesus said to them, "Why are you talking about having no bread? ...When I broke the five loaves for the five thousand, how many baskets full of broken pieces did you collect?" They said to him, "Twelve." "And the seven for the four thousand, how many baskets full of broken pieces did you collect?" And they said to him, "Seven." Then he said to them, "Do you not yet understand?" Mark 8:17, 19-21 (NRSV)

11-9
Money

The love of money was viewed by Jesus and His early followers as a great evil. It shifts trust in our Father to trust in something else. It spoils our character. It corrupts our soul. It is a barrier to a pure heart. The Father knows what we need. He is our Provider. We are content with Him and what He supplies. We love Him more than what He gives us!

"Make sure that your character is free from the love of money, being content with what you have; for He Himself has said, "I WILL NEVER DESERT YOU, NOR WILL I EVER FORSAKE YOU," so that we confidently say, "THE LORD IS MY HELPER, I WILL NOT BE AFRAID. WHAT WILL MAN DO TO ME?" Hebrews 13:5-6 (NASB)

11-10
A Grain of Wheat

A little grain of wheat said to itself, "I am all alone in the world and do not want to be alone anymore." A voice from above said, "Then die!" A man said, "I have kept my life for myself and I am tired of it. I want more!" A voice from above said, "Then die!" Give it up and it is given back. Give it away and you have it richer and fuller. Die, be buried, and you will have life. The world thinks it is crazy. But it is the hidden secret of real life.

"Listen carefully: Unless a grain of wheat is buried in the ground, dead to the world, it is never any more than a grain of wheat. But if it is buried, it sprouts and reproduces itself many times over. In the same way, anyone who holds on to life just as it is destroys that life. But if you let it go, reckless in your love, you'll have it forever, real and eternal." John 12:24-25 (The Message)

11-11
Believer Actions

"But you, beloved, building yourselves up on your most holy faith, praying in the Holy Spirit, keep yourselves in the love of God, waiting anxiously for the mercy of our Lord Jesus Christ to eternal life" (Jude 1:20-21). The Christian life is active and participatory. It is a life built on the "the faith once delivered to the saints". It prays in and with the holy-making Spirit. It is not drifting from, but keeping itself in the love of God. It is waiting anxiously for a coming mercy.

11-12
Re-present Messiah

The prophet must not speak when God has not spoken. The teacher must not teach what is false about God. The disciple must not misrepresent his Master by his actions. Instead, we are representatives, living images of our Lord by our daily living. A self-serving ambassador is a contradiction. Spirituality that brings us to self-centeredness is corrupting. That which re-presents our Lord is healthy for us and healing to those touched by it.

So Jesus said to them again, "Peace be with you; as the Father has sent Me, I also send you." And when He had said this, He breathed on them and said* to them, "Receive the Holy Spirit." John 20:21-22 (NASB)

11-13
Servant God!

God wants to express His life to His world by living under your skin, in your heart, out of your fingertips, through deeds of compassion, by your helping hands, every day. The Servant God of the Universe, revealed by Jesus, wants you in His servant kingdom, bringing healing, deliverance and setting things right in His world. Our servant actions confess our allegiance to His Lordship.

"Whoever wants to be great must become a servant....That is what the Son of Man has done: He came to serve, not be served—and then to give away His life in exchange for the many who are held hostage." Matthew 20:26-28 (The Message)

11-14
Unaltered Word

I fear that some of the messages from God have been altered by my immaturity, reality, agenda or problem of the moment. Lord, teach me to hear as You really are, undiluted by the stuff I bring to the conversation. Keep using your Word, Jesus, as the great corrective in my life to what I thought You were saying. May I apply Your pure Word but never twist it! May I hear to obey! Spirit of the Word, please come to my aid. Amen!

"The words of the LORD are pure words; As silver tried in a furnace on the earth, refined seven times." Psalms 12:6 (NASB)

11-15
Let Him Glow

There was a hidden glory in the Old Testament that the people were afraid to see so Moses put a veil over his face. In Jesus, we behold "the glory of the only begotten of the Father." We are changed by that vision to be bearers of glory. It is not our glory but His. Not ours to keep, but to "let it shine." We hide ourselves by humility and self-denial, but we do not hide Him. Beholding His glory transforms us. We radiate His light to the darkness.

"But we all, with unveiled face, beholding as in a mirror the glory of the Lord, are being transformed into the same image from glory to glory, just as from the Lord, the Spirit." 2 Corinthians 3:18 (NASB)

11-16
Potential

Good parents want their children to reach their full potential. Our Heavenly Father wants that for us. He wants to see all the ways that He has gifted us blossom. He is more than involved in the process through grace. This grace enables us to become. It is Spirit energy at work in us. He leads into His perfect vision for us. We can't always know what He is doing. We are blessed by our Lord to become. Stay in the process!

"And he took the children in his arms, put his hands on them and blessed them." Mark 10:16 (NIV)

11-17
God's Heart

We discover the heart of God in the cross. We look inside and find it to be a heart of compassion spilling out in love toward us. We find it to be filled with loving-kindness and mercy, a fountain of grace to the undeserving. It was in the heart of God all along, even before Calvary, but it was the dying Son who revealed the fullness of God's heart. His loving heart wants to be intimately connected to our hearts. This is the embrace we long for!

"For God so loved the world, that He gave His only begotten Son, that whoever believes in Him shall not perish, but have eternal life." John 3:16 (NASB)

11-18
God Moments

If we could only see, God is at work in everyone's life. God communicates to those who will hear. Word radiates from God like rays do from the sun. Everything in the universe speaks about Him. He also speaks to us in *God moments* that let us know that Someone *up there* cares about us. These moments remind us that we are part of a bigger plan. We miss some of them because we aren't looking. See them and be thankful
.
"In everything give thanks; for this is God's will for you in Christ Jesus." 1 Thessalonians 5:18 (NASB)

11-19
Beauty

God cares about beauty. Take a look at flowers, trees, birds, fish, mammals, mountains, valleys, rivers, etc. The colors and detailed arrangements are mind boggling. God makes beautiful things and you are one of them. Don't let the culture or the Accuser tell you that you are not. Surrender to His shaping. Your Father is still creating you and He treasures your unique beauty.

"He has made everything beautiful in its time." Ecclesiastes 3:11a (NIV)

11-20
Grace to Be

Paul wrote: "But by the grace of God I am what I am." (I Corinthians 15:10). The quality of your God relationship gives you true identity. The culture would like to tell you who you are and what you were meant to be. The Accuser's voice uses smooth arguments to move you toward the destructive. To really know the Father, as He has been revealed to us by the Son, is to find yourself and the grace to be what you were meant to be.

11-21
Perseverance As Faith

Life can be crushing sometimes. Its weight can be nearly overwhelming. You are forced to deal with things that you can't avoid. The pain won't go away. Faith, in these times, may be nothing more than perseverance and unwillingness to despair and quit. You put one foot in front of the other and go on even when it hurts more than anyone can imagine. You will make it through the dark valley.

"They say to me all day long, "Where is your God? Why are you in despair, O my soul? And why have you become disturbed within me? Hope in God, for I shall yet praise Him, The help of my countenance and my God" Psalms 42:10b-11 (NASB).

11-22
Voiceless Worship

Though we worship with our voices, there is a kind of worship without a voice. It is the worship of giving our bodies to God as living sacrifices of servanthood (Romans 12:1-2). It is obedience to the teachings of Jesus which He said is a mark of our love. Voiced praise without action is cheap worship. Real worship requires a life of voiceless actions and costly sacrifice. Worship will cost us everything, but love for our merciful Lord does not count it pain.

King David said to Araunah who had offered a free place and free stuff for worship, "No, but I will surely buy it from you for a price, for I will not offer burnt offerings to the LORD my God which cost me nothing." So David bought the threshing floor and the oxen for fifty shekels of silver.   2 Samuel 24:24 (NASB)

11-23
Be Still and Know

Talking reinforces or clarifies what we already know. Listening enables us to hear another person's thoughts, feel their presence and experience that person. So it is with praying! By creating the art of being still and listening, we come to know our Heavenly Father. It fosters a deep inner knowing beyond words. It gives us the union with God for which we hunger. It gives us all the resources we need to meet life!

"Be still, and know that I am God; I will be exalted among the nations, I will be exalted in the earth." Psalms 46:10 (NIV)

11-24
Shepherd Care

Our Shepherd loves all His sheep. Black ones, too. Crippled ones. Broken ones. Grieving ones. Lonely and discouraged ones. He embraces the abused. He binds up wounds. He anoints. He heals. He feeds so we do not lack. He counts us because we count. He comes for us when we stray from the fold. He throws a party when we come back. He laid down His life for us ragtag sheep. He really cares! I mean really cares!

"The LORD is my shepherd, I shall not want." Psalms 23:1 (NASB)

11-25
Truth Discovery

Our ideas that we think are original are not as original as we think they are. Things come to us from the energy of a God who expresses Himself in the universe. Someone said that "science is thinking the thoughts of God after Him." This is certainly true of spiritual truth. Truth is to be discovered and is not generated or created by us. We bow to it. It judges us. Jesus spoke the truth and He is Truth. This frontier never runs out. He is inexhaustible!

"The elder to the chosen lady and her children, whom I love in truth; and not only I, but also all who know the truth, for the sake of the truth which abides in us and will be with us forever" 2 John 1:1-2 (NASB).

11-26
Dry

Sometimes God cuts us off from all things so that we can depend on Him alone. We like props. These can become God-substitutes. There are times when we feel and sense His presence. There are times we don't. He is not absent from us. He is maturing us. We learn to walk by confident trusting faith and not for the sweets He may give. Dry times make our roots reach deeper. These times result in their own maturing sweetness.

"We walk by faith and not sight." 2 Corinthians 5:7 (NASB)

11-27
Persuasion

The good news of the kingdom of God is about persuasion and not compulsion. Persons cannot be brought into the kingdom by force, manipulation or other non-Holy-Spirit methods. The Son and the Spirit are sent to the world to draw the world back to God, its rightful King. We are Messiah's ambassadors sent to persuade God's enemies to become His friends. Actions of love and grace are the King's chosen way to do this.

"And he entered the synagogue and continued speaking out boldly for three months, reasoning and persuading them about the kingdom of God." Acts 19:8 (NASB)

11-28
Ready Obedience

The whole of the Biblical story suggests that God wants an interactive relationship with His creatures. This does not work when one is the active talker and the other is the passive listener. We may bring a request to God and hear Him saying to us, "What are you going to do about it?" We give God our 'to do' list, but keep His list for us out of sight and out of mind. Lord, teach me how to be a better coworker and servant with ready obedience.

Now the LORD came and stood there, calling as before, "Samuel! Samuel!" And Samuel said, "Speak, for your servant is listening." 1 Samuel 3:10 (NRSV)

11-29
Off Center

We are all born with narcissistic tendencies. Western culture encourages it. It is the worldliness we must flee. It is the source of evil. It is the off centeredness of the self that must be crucified. It is an inner anti-Christ to Christ's inner kingdom. We need the eyes of the Spirit to truly see ourselves so we can see what needs to die and what needs to be disciplined. It is that for which we need to repent and cry for a deep cleansing work.

"But if you have bitter jealousy and selfish ambition in your heart, do not be arrogant and so lie against the truth. This wisdom is not that which comes down from above, but is earthly, natural, demonic. For where jealousy and selfish ambition exist, there is disorder and every evil thing" James 3:14-16 (NASB).

11-30
Receiving Jesus

"He took a small child and stood it in the middle of them. Then he hugged the child" (KNT) and said, "Whoever receives one child like this in My name receives Me" (Mark 9:36-37). Have you received Jesus lately? No, I don't mean conversion! I mean, have you received those who have no status or standing, the unloved, ignored, and neglected of our world. To receive them is to receive Jesus. Father, help me not miss another chance to hug Jesus.

12-1
Depend On The Lord

Depending on our own human power gets us into trouble. I can't depend only on myself and get it right. I need God's power to direct and energize me. Being prayerfully open to grace and sensitive to the moment trains me away from acting or reacting without grace. If I depend on me, I will fail. If I depend on the Lord, He will help me. Lord, may I learn to live in such a way that complete trust in You is as natural as breathing.

This is what the LORD says: "Cursed is the one who trusts in man, who depends on flesh for His strength and whose heart turns away from the LORD. He will be like a bush in the wastelands; he will not see prosperity when it comes. He will dwell in the parched places of the desert, in a salt land where no one lives. But blessed is the man who trusts in the LORD, whose confidence is in him." Jeremiah 17:5-7 (NIV)

12-2
There is More

It is so easy to focus on favorite facets of truth. God has more to say than that to which we restrict Him. Our focus and tuning limits our ability to hear. We are comfortable with what we know or think we know. God has truth, the depths of which we have not plumbed nor have we sailed its seas. Unfold your sails. Truth will take you where it will. With your open eyes, ears and heart, you will be enriched by broad horizons of breathtaking beauty.

"The heavens declare the glory of God; the skies proclaim the work of his hands. Day after day they pour forth speech; night after night they display knowledge. There is no speech or language where their voice is not heard. Their voice goes out into all the earth, their words to the ends of the world." Psalms 19:1-4 (NIV)

12-3
Sifted

Temptations have a way of sifting our hearts. It attempts to pull us away from God's mission for our lives with more attractive ones. Yielding to temptation is sin. There are some yieldings that are so subtle only thoughtful reflection will reveal where we crossed the line. Temptation finds our character for what it is and our response to it makes us stronger or weaker. The test will reveal who our Lord really is.

"Satan has demanded *permission* to sift you like wheat; but I have prayed for you, that your faith may not fail." Luke 22:31-32 (NASB)

12-4
Love Does

Love is as love does. It is an attitude expressed as action. We commit money, time and attention to what we truly love. Stewardship says the Lord owns me and all I own. Consumerism is at war with stewardship. Due to our undisciplined way of handling time and money leaves pitifully little given to God's work. This reveals what we love. Your heart follows your treasure, "For where your treasure is, there your heart will be also" (Matthew 6:21).

12-5
Integrated Faith

If you belong to the Lord, you cannot be comfortable with relationships and life compartments that conveniently leave Him out. If you have back-shelved the Lord for fear you will lose someone or something, your divided heart has just been revealed. Our faith affects every action, relationship and compartment or it is phony. Our faith, when intentionally and holistically integrated into our lives, brings peace and wholeness.

"I will give them a heart to know Me, for I am the LORD; and they will be My people, and I will be their God, for they will return to Me with their whole heart." Jeremiah 24:7 (NASB)

12-6
A Love Like His

We want God to be as upset with our enemies as we are. He wants us to love them like He does. God does not select certain categories of people marked for non-love as we do. His love knows no boundaries. God, who is love dwelling within us, sets our hearts to loving what He loves. This is the DNA of God's children and the evidence that He dwells in us. Lord, may our love for others be of the same kind as the love You poured out on us.

"Dear friends, let us love one another, for love comes from God. Everyone who loves has been born of God and knows God. Whoever does not love does not know God, because God is love. This is how God showed His love among us: He sent His one and only Son into the world that we might live through him. This is love: not that we loved God, but that he loved us and sent His Son as an atoning sacrifice for our sins. Dear friends, since God so loved us, we also ought to love one another. No one has ever seen God; but if we love one another, God lives in us and his love is made complete in us." 1 John 4:7-12 (NIV)

12-7
Life for You

Sin kills because it is poison. Sin's salary is death (Romans 6:23). This is why your Father is calling you out of it and away from it. It is not to spoil your fun, but to save your fun. It is not to hurt you but to help you. Your Father passionately desires you to have Life. He sent His Son to rescue you from death enabling you to become a partaker of heaven's Life, even while in this world, through the resurrection of Messiah Jesus from the dead.

"This grace was given to us in Messiah Jesus before the ages began, but it has now been revealed through the appearing of our Deliverer Messiah Jesus, who abolished death and brought life and immortality to light through the good news" (2 Timothy 1:9b-10).

12-8
Eat Better

When we change what and how we eat, our long term physical health changes. To be healthy, we need to acquire new tastes for what our body truly needs. The same is true of spiritual food. We look for what we already know tastes good to us. We like fast-food worship and snack-food reading. A juvenile desire for spiritual sweets produces juvenile Christians. The substantial meat of God's Word will mature us into spiritual adults.

"And I, brethren, could not speak to you as to spiritual men, but as to men of flesh, as to infants in Christ. I gave you milk to drink, not solid food; for you were not yet able to receive it. Indeed, even now you are not yet able." 1 Corinthians 3:1-2 (NASB)

12-9
He Knows Us

Parents sometimes know their own children more than the children know or even can know themselves. Good parents' advice and direction draws on the personal knowledge they have of the child. Our Father knows us individually; out of His perfect wisdom He guides us. His Word and His Spirit direct us toward holy character. He knows the path each us needs to take to get us there. He does not slumber nor sleep but is eternally vigilant in His purposes for us.

"I will lead the blind by a way they do not know, In paths they do not know I will guide them. I will make darkness into light before them And rugged places into plains. These are the things I will do, And I will not leave them undone." Isaiah 42:16 (NASB)

12-10
Irreducible

We have impoverished the faith by reading our shallow understandings into rich biblical words. We have reduced salvation to a formula that insures heaven when we die. Our reductionism aims at having a system we can control, and one that saves us from sacrifice and discipleship. Additionally, it leaves us absent at God's rich truth banquet. Our dynamic relationship with God is too wonderful not to be tasted and too expansive to be reduced.

"O LORD, our Lord, How majestic is Your name in all the earth, Who have displayed Your splendor above the heavens! Psalms 8:1 (NASB)

12-11
Inspiration

We must digest and assimilate the food we eat for it to give health to our bodies. It is possible to read biblical truth without digestion and assimilation. To avoid this, we must think about what we are reading, even *chew on it.* Keep a teachable spirit, bowing to the authority of God's word. Look carefully. Listen obediently. Let it retrain our behaviors. We need the Spirit who inspired the words in the beginning to give fresh inspiration to our hearts.

"All Scripture is inspired by God and profitable for teaching, for reproof, for correction, for training in righteousness; so that the man of God may be adequate, equipped for every good work" (2 Timothy 3:16-17, NASB).

12-12
Our Asking

God is not interested is answering prayers that will hinder our growth and maturity.   Not being a permissive Parent, He says, "No", for our good and makes it stick. He is not panicked by our insistence. He listens to all of our prayers.   Often times the answer comes in changing the character of the asking. As we mature, our asking matures. Lovingly trust the Father and patiently wait for His answer, in His way, and in His time.

"For the LORD God is a sun and shield; The LORD gives grace and glory; No good thing does He withhold from those who walk uprightly. O LORD of hosts, How blessed is the man who trusts in You!" Psalms 84:11-12 (NASB)

12-13
Taste the Lord

Truly tasting and appreciating the diverse foods God has given us is a way of showing gratitude.   The

Psalmist used tasting as an analogy for relishing the Lord. The manner in which we eat our food can be an act of worship to God, "who richly supplies us all things to enjoy" (I Timothy 6:17). The forethought of the Creator gave us innumerable varieties of delicious food to tell us of His love and care for us. To thoughtfully eat is to taste our loving incarnate Lord.

"O taste and see that the LORD is good; How blessed is the man who takes refuge in Him! Psalms 34:10 (NASB)

12-14
No Payback

"To sum up, all of you be harmonious, sympathetic, brotherly, kindhearted, and humble in spirit; not returning evil for evil or insult for insult, but giving a blessing instead; for you were called for the very purpose that you might inherit a blessing" (1 Peter 3:8-9). We are prone to respond in kind. Christians are instructed in another way. Jesus taught that when insulted, cursed or mistreated, to respond with a blessing. Those who will are promised a blessing.

12-15
Messiah is Our Master

The Lordship of Christ is the foundation of Christian faith. Jude wrote about those who had turned grace into a license to sin (licentiousness). This is a denial of our Lord and Master since sin itself seeks mastery over us. Grace does not give us permission to sin, but is the inner power of the Spirit giving us victory, which we cannot achieve on our own. Living out of the energy of grace both demonstrates faith and contends for it.

"I felt the necessity to write to you appealing that you contend earnestly for the faith which was once for all handed down to the saints. For certain persons have crept in unnoticed, those who were long beforehand marked out for this condemnation, ungodly persons who turn the grace of our God into licentiousness *(license for immorality* NIV) and deny our only Master and Lord, Jesus Christ." Jude 1:3b-4 (NASB)

12-16
Temple Hospitality

You are a sanctuary in which God dwells. "Do you not know that you are a temple of God and that the Spirit of God dwells in you?" (1 Corinthians 3:16). Give hospitality to the indwelling Spirit, worshipfully welcome Him. Sing to Him. Tend the lamp in your inner house of prayer. "Pray without ceasing" (I Thessalonians 5:17). Never let the incense stop ascending. Give sacrifices on your altar. Partake of the holy food He brings to you and be thankful.

12-17
Thought Life

Our thoughts can "defile us" (Mark 7:23). What is in the mind and heart spills out to either bless or curse us and those we touch. We are the expression of our thoughts. We are like the world when we think like the world. The Holy Spirit is at work in us to transform our thought life. He helps us to think right about God, ourselves and our neighbor. The discipline and grace of the Spirit changes our thinking enabling us to bless the world.

"And do not be conformed to this world, but be transformed by the renewing of your mind, so that you may prove what the will of God is, that which is good and acceptable and perfect" Romans 12:2 (NASB).

12-18
Servant Initiative

Our Master wants servants who walk through open doors of service. He wants those who will see opportunities of ministry others miss. Seasoned servants know how to see what needs to be done and do it. They do not wait for a command or special guidance. They have learned over time what their Master desires and move into action. Servants who take initiative to do more than the minimal are rewarded.

"Would he thank the servant because he did what he was told to do? So you also, when you have done everything you were told to do, should say, 'We are unworthy servants; we have only done our duty'" Luke 17:9-10 (NIV).

12-19
Willing His Will

To use our will against God's clearly revealed will, destroys freedom and leads to bondage. It keeps us turned inward instead of upward. It stops worship. It works against grace instead of with grace. A will tuned to the will of God, creates harmony in our whole being. Lord, grant us the grace to will what You will. May we live so close to You, that it becomes natural to know Your will and to will it without reluctance. Amen!

"Teach me to do Your will, for You are my God; Let Your good Spirit lead me on level ground" Ps 143:10 (NASB).

12-20
Shadows and Light

We tend to let our sorrows silence our joys and overshadow our blessings. We must not spend our time looking down at the shadow, it only magnifies the sorrow. Turn toward the Light! There is always light behind a shadow. If we only see our problems and grief, we lose perspective. There is an intimate communion we discover with our Beloved walking with us through the shadowlands. It is the intimacy of walking with Light.

Job said, "When His lamp shone over my head, And by His light I walked through darkness," (Job 29:3). Jesus said, "I am the Light of the world; he who follows Me will not walk in the darkness, but will have the Light of life." John 8:12 (ESV)

12-21
Forgiven to Live

Having difficulty forgiving yourself of some past offense? Then picture yourself in this story: "Jesus said to the paralyzed man, 'Son, your sins are forgiven...I say to you, get up, pick up your pallet and go home'" (Mark 2:5,11). To us it is, "Son/Daughter your sins are forgiven, get up and get on with your life." Holding to forgiven sin paralyzes us. Jesus said, "*Forgiven!*" It is done! Thank you Jesus! I am forgiven to really live!

"My sin- O the bliss of this glorious thought- My sin not in part, but the whole- is nailed to His cross, and I bear it no more! Praise the Lord, praise the Lord, O my soul!" -Hymn "It is Well with My Soul".

12-22
Eye of the Needle

Jesus spoke of "how hard it is" to enter the kingdom of God, especially for the rich. The difficulty of entering the kingdom is not made possible by reducing the demands of our Lord's gospel with easy formulas and cheap grace. His call still stands: "leave all and follow." "How hard it is!" but God makes possible the impossible. His grace enables embracing the cross as a "living sacrifice". That's how we all get through the eye of the needle.

"The disciples were amazed at His words. But Jesus answered again and said to them, 'Children, how hard it is to enter the kingdom of God! It is easier for a camel to go through the eye of a needle than for a rich man to enter the kingdom of God.' They were even more astonished and said to Him, 'Then who can be saved?' Looking at them, Jesus *said, 'With people it is impossible, but not with God; for all things are possible with God'" Mark 10:24-27 (NASB)

12-23
Loving the Lord

To fully embrace the Lordship of Christ, is foundational to a loving connection with our Lord. If I contest His Lordship and take things into my own hands, I have thrown a kink into the love relationship. If He is Lord, and He is; if we are His servants, and we are; then whenever He calls, wherever He sends, or whatever He requires is okay. We love it that way. One mark of maturity is that we enjoy letting the Lord be Lord.

"So choose life in order that you may live,...by loving the Lord your God, by obeying His voice, and by holding fast to Him; for this is your life and the length of your days." Deuteronomy 30:19b-20a (NASB)

12-24
Sharing His Nature

The redeemed have been given "His precious and magnificent promises, so that by them you may become partakers (sharers) of the divine nature" (II Peter 1:4). That I, a former slave of corruption, would be invited to a union close enough to *partake of the divine nature*, is a mind boggling promise. By incarnation, He became one with us so that we might become one with Him. He partook of our nature permitting us to partake of His nature.

"His divine power has given us everything needed for life and godliness, through the knowledge of him who called us by his own glory and goodness. Thus he has given us, through these things, his precious and very great promises, so that through them you may escape from the corruption that is in the world because of lust, and may become participants of the divine nature" (2 Peter 1:3-4 NRSV).

12-25
God's Forbearance

It is difficult to be patient with ourselves. We are an incomplete work in progress. We need to give ourselves grace, or better said, live in the wonderful present grace of our Lord. Our false ideas of a perfectionist God who can't be pleased needs to be replaced with a vision of one who surrounds us with lovingkindness, grace and mercy. His forbearance is astonishing. He cheers our growth and patiently anticipates our fruit.

"He who trusts in the LORD, lovingkindness shall surround him" Ps 32:10b (NASB).

12-26
Listen for the Spirit

The Bible was written by humans like us who were inspired by the Holy Spirit. The Holy Spirit still speaks to humans like us through Scripture. It is more than law, principles and doctrines. We read its great narrative with all the sub narratives and see God's hand at work. We hear in those stories a Spirit inspired message for us. For this reason, we must never separate prayer from reading and the Spirit from listening.

"He who has an ear, let him hear what the Spirit says to the churches" Rev 3:22 (NASB).

12-27
Let Your Heart Sing

A soul without a song is pathetic thing to behold. God's people have always sung. Facing Golgotha, Jesus leads the disciples in a song. He is our song. The indwelling Spirit inspires music in the heart. Sing when you don't feel like it, and the song will change how you feel. Even alone, open a hymn book and sing aloud. If you don't know the tune, read the poem. Inspired songs energize and motivate the heart. You need a song!

"Be filled with the Spirit. Speak to one another with psalms, hymns and spiritual songs. Sing and make music in your heart to the Lord, always giving thanks to God the Father for everything, in the name of our Lord Jesus Christ" Ephesians 5:18b-20 (NIV).

12-28
Move On

It is not possible to release something I need to release if I am still obsessing about it. Hanging on to my forgiven sins is itself a sin of unbelief. If God has *let go* of my offenses, then I need to get on God's page. God is moving us to better plans for the rest of our lives, and here I am looking backward. Lord, teach me to *release what You have released* and to live this moment in the assurance faith gives.

"For I will be merciful toward their iniquities, and I will remember their sins no more" Hebrews 8:12 (NRSV).

12-29
Mutual Indwelling

"God is love. Whoever lives in love lives in God, and God in him" (1 John 4:16b NIV). God dwells in love for it is the perfect expression of who He is. Where real agape is, God is. God is hidden in love. God is revealed in love. His Spirit pours love into our hearts (Romans 5:5). We are given love to bless the world by loving. Living in the love of God and the love of God living in me is the evidence that God and I are abiding in each other.

12-30
Seed Power

Never underestimate the transforming power of a seed planted in a human heart. A verse, a sermon, a book, a witness, or a quiet time can produce a seed inside us that creates transformation. In our hearts today, we have seeds planted that have not yet sprouted and broken out of the ground of our souls. Holy Spirit, tend these precious seeds that need to germinate! Oh Heart Gardener, we yield to You!

"And those are the ones on whom seed was sown on the good soil; and they hear the word and accept it and bear fruit, thirty, sixty, and a hundredfold," Jesus in Mark 4:20 (NASB).

12-31
Faithfulness

Faithfulness is tenacious faith that holds on to the Lord no matter what. It does not shrink back from confidence in its Lord when tested. It believes in One who can work His purposes when everything seems to the contrary. This faithfulness looks for the path God has created through an unchartered wilderness. It cannot know all the details so it commits that also. It is a faith that is conscious of One who loves us, holds us and will never fail us!

"For yet 'in a very little while, the one who is coming will come and will not delay; but my righteous one will live by faith. My soul takes no pleasure in anyone who shrinks back.' But we are not among those who shrink back and so are lost, but among those who have faith and so are saved" Hebrews 10:37-39 (NRSV).

Benediction

The LORD bless you and keep you;
The LORD make His face shine upon you,
And be gracious to you;
The LORD lift up His countenance upon you,
And give you peace.

Numbers 6:24-26 (NKJV)